I Am a Fugitive from a Chain Gang

Wisconsin/Warner Bros. Screenplay Series

I Am a Fugitive from a Chain Gang

Edited with an introduction by

John E. O'Connor

Published for the Wisconsin Center for Film and Theater Research by
The University of Wisconsin Press

Published 1981

The University of Wisconsin Press
114 North Murray Street
Madison, Wisconsin 53715

The University of Wisconsin Press, Ltd.
1 Gower Street
London WC1E 6HA, England

First printing

Printed in the United States of America

For LC CIP information see the colophon

ISBN 0-299-08750-6 cloth; 0-299-08754-9 paper

Publication of this volume has been assisted by a grant from
The Brittingham Fund, Inc.

Contents

Foreword 7
Tino Balio

Introduction: Warners Finds Its Social Conscience 9
John E. O'Connor

Illustrations 45

I Am a Fugitive from a Chain Gang 61

Notes to the Screenplay 188

Production Credits 195

Cast 196

Inventory 197

Foreword

In donating the Warner Film Library to the Wisconsin Center for Film and Theater Research in 1969, along with the RKO and Monogram film libraries and UA corporate records, United Artists created a truly great resource for the study of American film. Acquired by United Artists in 1957, during a period when the major studios sold off their films for use on television, the Warner library is by far the richest portion of the gift, containing eight hundred sound features, fifteen hundred short subjects, nineteen thousand still negatives, legal files, and press books, in addition to screenplays for the bulk of the Warner Brothers product from 1930 to 1950. For the purposes of this project, the company has granted the Center whatever publication rights it holds to the Warner films. In so doing, UA has provided the Center another opportunity to advance the cause of film scholarship.

Our goal in publishing these Warner Brothers screenplays is to explicate the art of screenwriting during the thirties and forties, the so-called Golden Age of Hollywood. In preparing a critical introduction and annotating the screenplay, the editor of each volume is asked to cover such topics as the development of the screenplay from its source to the final shooting script, differences between the final shooting script and the release print, production information, exploitation and critical reception of the film, its historical importance, its directorial style, and its position within the genre. He is also encouraged to go beyond these guidelines to incorporate supplemental information concerning the studio system of motion picture production.

We could set such an ambitious goal because of the richness of the script files in the Warner Film Library. For many film titles, the files might contain the property (novel, play, short story, or original story idea), research materials, variant drafts of scripts (from story outline to treatment to shooting script), post-production items such as press books and dialogue continuities, and legal records (details of the acquisition of the property, copyright registration, and contracts with actors and directors). Editors of the Wisconsin/Warner Bros. Screenplay Series receive copies of all the materials, along with prints of the films (the most authoritative ones available for reference purposes), to use in preparing the introductions and annotating the final shooting scripts.

In the process of preparing the screenplays for publication, typographical errors were corrected, punctuation and capitalization were modernized, and the format was redesigned to facilitate readability.

Unless otherwise specified, the photographs are frame enlargements taken from a 35-mm print of the film provided by United Artists.

In 1977 Warner Brothers donated the company's production records and distribution records to the University of Southern California and Princeton University, respectively. These materials are now available to researchers and complement the contents of the Warner Film Library donated to the Center by United Artists.

Tino Balio
General Editor

Introduction
Warners Finds Its Social Conscience

John E. O'Connor

Such films of social consciousness as *I Am a Fugitive from a Chain Gang, Heroes for Sale* (1933), *Wild Boys of the Road* (1933), *Black Fury* (1935), *Black Legion* (1937), and *They Won't Forget* (1937) did more than pluck at the public's heartstrings. They all implied that forbidding forces were at work that were wholly unpredictable and yet capable of overtaking the hopes and ambitions of an individual. To some observers of the Depression these factors were obvious and inevitable ramifications of the American capitalist system, but to others they seemed completely capricious. Much of the literature of the 1930s depicts a people trying to come to grips with the realization that such forces were robbing them of the capacity to shape their own destinies. Business leaders had long known that the days of the heroic entrepreneur were gone, and intellectuals had questioned for decades whether there was any room for free will in their explanations of men's actions. It was in the 1930s, however, that popular authors such as James T. Farrell, John Dos Passos, John Steinbeck, and others convinced many average Americans that their way in life was more likely to be determined by giant impersonal forces in society than by any decisions they could make on their own. This message was brought home unrelentingly by *I Am a Fugitive from a Chain Gang*, the first of the Depression decade films to focus so closely on a factual story of ordinary people in such desperate distress.

Since the time of its release in 1932, *Chain Gang* has earned a reputation as one of the few Hollywood products that can be directly associated with social change—not only a shift in popular attitudes but a revision of government policy. According to film historians, the reform of the southern chain gang system can be attributed to the public outrage generated by this movie. Jack Warner, Darryl Zanuck, and Mervyn LeRoy have since taken personal credit for creating this hard-hitting document of social criticism. Warner said it was "the first sermon I had ever put on film."[1] To many people at the Warners studio at the time, however, who thought that the most reliable formula for making successful movies in the early 1930s was to stick with escapist themes and appeal to the broadest possible audience, it seemed a terrible mistake to make a film like *Chain Gang*, which appeared more to preach about social injustice than to entertain.

It was Darryl Zanuck whose determination and faith in his own judgment brought the studio to run the risk of filming the chain gang story. As will be explained, Zanuck also had considerable influence upon the adaptation of the story for the screen. In retrospect we can name at least three reasons that Zanuck gambled on such a project. First, recent prison pictures had done very well. Movies such as *The Big House* (1930), *Up the River* (1930), *Ladies of the Big House* (1931), *The Criminal Code* (1931), and others had proven the prison theme to be a salable one. The idea of a movie about a chain gang promised to build on the style of gritty realism established by the very successful run in 1931 of films on gangsterism, including *The Public Enemy, City Streets*, and *The Secret Six.* (Producers at Warner Brothers weren't the only ones to predict a ready market for a chain gang picture. At the same moment, RKO was preparing to film *Hell's Highway*, which reached first-run theaters just six weeks before *I Am a Fugitive from a Chain Gang*.) Second, the studio was able to call upon special talents, Paul Muni for the leading role and Mervyn LeRoy for director. Muni had received rave reviews for his realistic portrayal of an Al Capone-like character in *Scarface*

1. Jack L. Warner, with Dean Jennings, *My First Hundred Years in Hollywood* (New York: Random House, 1964), p. 218. See also Arthur Knight, *The Liveliest Art: A Panoramic History of the Movies* (rev. ed; New York: Macmillan, 1978), p. 219, and his essay in *The Warner Bros. Golden Anniversary Book* (New York: Dell, 1973), p. 15; Mervyn LeRoy, as told to Dick Kleiner, *Mervyn LeRoy: Take One* (New York: Hawthorn, 1974), p. 111.

(1932), and LeRoy had to his credit Warners films of both the prison and gangster genre—*Numbered Men* (1930) and *Little Caesar* (1931).

Finally, the subject had had a lot of recent publicity. Robert Elliot Burns's escape from a Georgia chain gang, his rise to success and respectability as a Chicago businessman, his subsequent return to the chain gang, and his second escape had become well known to the American public. Twice in the preceding three years Burns's story had flashed across the national wire services: in 1929 when Chicago police seized him after his estranged wife had reported him to Georgia authorities and in 1930 when he made good his second escape. On each occasion the story drew headlines and sympathetic articles that concentrated on the inhumane conditions of life on the southern chain gang and characterized Burns as a solid, respectable citizen who had been grossly mistreated by the institutions of southern justice. Since then the story had been serialized in *True Detective Mysteries* magazine and was about to be published in book form by Vantage Press in New York.

Burns's account was a real human interest story, much of which had actually taken place in the seamy surroundings of underclass life in America. The tramps and hoboes, the flophouse hotels, the dirty corner diners, the petty criminals—all the character and scenic elements that had been invented by the imaginative minds of the Warners studio to make *The Public Enemy, Little Caesar,* and other popular films seem realistic—were matters of fact in the story of Robert E. Burns. And best of all, unlike Hollywood's Tommy Powers and Rico Bandello who had come to rather predictable conclusions, Burns had escaped from the chain gang to begin a crusade to clear his name, and the crusade was still going on as the film was being made. The fugitive remained at large all during the film's production, providing a gold mine for studio publicists. In fact, the biggest risks Burns took during all of his months in hiding from the law were involved with promotion of the movie. Within two months after the release of the film, he was arrested again, and a new spate of national headlines provided continuing, effective press coverage for the Warner Brothers hit of the season.

Because the actual story was so infused with human interest, and because the studio thought the supposed "truthfulness" of their presentation was an important selling point with the public, there could not be too much rearranging of the narrative that Burns had laid out himself. The basic story line of the film follows the one that Burns sold to Warners in February of 1932 for $12,500.[2] The book, written mostly in the first person, is plodding and episodic. The author's self-serving attempt to portray himself as the personification of traditional middle-class values shines through on every page. The Warner Brothers stable of writers was put to work on what should have been the relatively simple tasks of converting the plot into dialogue form, polishing the language and metaphor, and providing some basic continuity and pacing to an otherwise flat and lifeless narrative. Still, the screenwriters assigned to the project did make some interesting adaptations and transformations of characters and story elements.

In all, over the course of fifteen weeks, there were six stages in the evolution of the script: (1) the Outline, dated April 15, 1932, which amounted to a sixteen-page rendering of the framework of the Burns book; (2) the eighty-six-page Treatment, ten days later, by Brown Holmes; (3) the Screenplay by Sheridan Gibney; and (4) the Temporary script written by Gibney and Holmes together. At this point Darryl Zanuck stepped in with his own suggestions for tightening things up and clarifying characterizations and aspects of the plot. Zanuck called in Howard J. Green to put the work into its final form. There was another story conference with Zanuck's suggestions being spelled out in detail before (5) Green's Screenplay became (6) the Final shooting script, dated July 23, 1932, with last-minute changes added on July 28.

The film that eventually reached the screen has earned mention in almost every survey of American genre film. In addition to its commercial success and its artistic acclaim (Muni and the

2. Contract between Warner Brothers and Robert E. Burns, February 25, 1932, Warner Bros. Contract and Copyright File, United Artists Collection, Wisconsin Center for Film and Theater Research, Madison, Wisconsin.

Warners' sound department each won an Oscar for their work), the film is interesting because it directly addresses an obvious issue of social concern, because its dramatic conception and especially its inconclusive ending were so unusual, and because Paul Muni's powerful and intense performance even today, almost fifty years later, makes the viewing of the film a gripping experience.

Moreover, *I Am a Fugitive from a Chain Gang* is a valuable document for the study of popular values and attitudes in Depression America. Especially in its portrayal of the role of women and of the ambitions of middle-class Americans at the time, the film touched sensitive nerve centers in the national consciousness. In its aura of humanitarian concern the film suggested a new departure for Hollywood as a force for social reform. In its image of public officials as callous, self-indulgent, and self-serving bureaucrats who could not be moved to correct even the most obvious injustices, the film represented a criticism of current political leaders on every level of government. And in its unwavering characterization of an individual hopelessly entrapped by monstrous social forces that nobody seemed able to control, the movie played upon the innermost fears of Americans, many of whom felt unsure about how they would survive—how the society itself would survive—the vicissitudes of an economic depression the likes of which the nation had never before seen.

The Story of Robert E. Burns

According to Burns's book, *I Am a Fugitive from a Georgia Chain Gang!*, it all began in May 1919, with a young GI returning home from the battlefields of Europe. "My, how good it was to be alive," Burns wrote, "to be back in the good old U.S.A.—still whole and young, with life before me!" Like thousands of other former doughboys, however, his dreams soon began to fade. His girlfriend had not waited for him after all and, worse still, good jobs were almost impossible to find. The $50-per-week position he had held before the war was filled by someone else, and with veterans a drug on the market the best he could turn up was a job that paid a weekly $17.60. As resentment mounted he felt as though he had been a "sucker," going off to fight while the smart guys stayed home and "grew rich on war contracts." His brother's introduction to the book throws doubt on Burns's judgment by suggesting that when the young man returned from the war he was "nervously unstrung and mentally erratic—a typical shell-shock case." But a lot of returning vets must have agreed with Burns's perception of what they had been through: "The promises of the Y.M.C.A. secretaries and all the other 'fountain-pen soldiers' who promised us so much in the name of nation and the Government just before we'd go into action turned out to be the bunk. Just a lot of plain applesauce!"[3]

Frustrated, depressed, and faced with the options of taking a job at a fraction of what he thought he was worth or living on indefinitely with his mother and brother, Burns, in his own words, "became a hobo—just drifting along and around—here, there, anywhere." He was alone and broke in a flophouse in Atlanta, Georgia, in 1922 when he was approached by two petty crooks who tricked him into helping them rob a neighborhood grocery store. The trio was arrested minutes afterward, and for his unpremeditated role in a $5.80 holdup Burns was sentenced to six to ten years at hard labor in the Georgia chain gang system. Already a victim of unfortunate circumstances, he would discover that his troubles were only beginning.

Burns's book described his horrible experiences in the prison camps in detail: the iron shackles attached to his legs, the chains that restricted his movement every moment of the day and night, the vicious guards who apparently thought nothing of punching him in the jaw for wiping sweat from his brow without asking permission, the unchanging diet of corn pone and pig fat, the lack of the most basic sanitary facilities, the torturous labor that broke the spirits of the inmates as well as their bodies, and a workday that invariably ended with at least one of the prisoners being singled out for a bloody whipping on bare but-

3. Robert E. Burns, *I Am a Fugitive from a Georgia Chain Gang!* (New York: Vanguard, 1932), p. 38. This summary is based on that edition of the book.

tocks with a sturdy leather strap. Going beyond his own personal experiences, Burns traced the history of the Georgia penal system back to the post–Civil War period when a rising tide of lawlessness combined with the need to reconstruct the war-ravaged South and the absence of any funds for construction of adequate prison facilities. The result was a prison contract system, a legal alternative to slavery, in which individuals could contract with the state for a negotiable fee and take away a prisoner in chains to work on their farms or plantations until his term was up. The system became so blatantly corrupt, with poorly paid prison commissioners openly taking bribes, that after 1900 the rules were changed so that counties rather than individuals contracted for the prisoners' labor. Still the system remained barbaric and, as Burns emphasized, there was no pretense of rehabilitation. In his reaction to all this corruption and cruelty, Burns portrayed himself throughout as a typically respectable middle-class American. Admitting he had done wrong (even if under mitigating circumstances), he was willing to pay his debt to society. But after his first week in prison he decided that he could not survive six years of the brutalizing camps and vowed that he would either escape or die trying.

With the help of a black inmate who used a sledgehammer to bend the shackles so he could work them off his feet, Burns ran off on June 21, 1922. Running for miles through the woods, he eventually evaded the bloodhounds by splashing into a river and swimming downstream for several miles. In Atlanta, with every policeman on the lookout for him, Burns barely escaped recognition in a barber shop, then luckily stumbled into a fleabag hotel that turned out to have a manager who had finished his term on the same chain gang just a few weeks before. With his help and that of a young prostitute who idolized Burns for his intention to live "the 'straight and narrow' instead of 'the free and easy' path," the escapee found his way north to Chicago—though not without a few close calls with the authorities.

Burns's book told about his work for the next seven years, first as a laborer and later as a real estate manager and magazine publisher. The personification of bourgeois values, he saved his money and eventually found the self-confidence necessary to make something of his life. But he still was not really free. Despite the care he took to keep his real identity a secret, the landlady of a rooming house he stayed in had been smitten with him, and in scrutinizing his mail she learned about his past in a letter from his brother in New Jersey. The woman was Hispanic and a divorcee, forty years old, dark haired, short and stout, very emotional, and very much in love with Burns. She threatened him with exposure if he did not marry her. Burns tried to explain that he did not and could not ever love her. As he plaintively (and tritely) put it to her, "Love is something you have to feel." In the end, though, he bowed to her insistence. The match did have its advantages. Her family had saved enough money to buy some real estate and set them up as apartment house managers. Burns poured that income into his dream of becoming a publisher, and within a year he had established *The Greater Chicago Magazine.* It was a struggle, Burns explained, soliciting advertisers all by himself and lecturing to civic groups three or four nights a week to build up a reputation. But the hard work paid off and he became recognized, to use his own words, as "both an honor and an asset to Chicago."

Meanwhile, his marriage was troubled. Burns and his wife were never close in a romantic way, and as Burns achieved success they grew further apart. The trouble reached a climax when he finally found someone whom he did love. Hollywood couldn't have dreamed up anything better. She was a waitress and a taxi dancer with ambitions to become a concert violinist. Before breaking the news to his wife, they set up a love nest where he would retire at the end of a busy day to have her serenade him on a violin. When he did ask his wife for a divorce, it did not take her long to get steamed up and flash off a letter to the Georgia authorities.

It was May 1929 and, as young people danced the Charleston and the stock market flirted with disaster, Burns's story grabbed national headlines. After his arrest, dozens of Chicago's business leaders came to his defense, offering legal and financial support. The Chicago police chief offered to help him evade extradition, and it seemed as though the governor of Illinois might bend to political pressure and refuse to send him back to prison in the South. But before a decision could be made, Burns did the most unlikely thing imaginable. After making sure that his lover would wait for him, he agreed to return to Georgia voluntarily on the premise that he would not be reassigned to a chain gang and that the prison commission would see to his parole within ninety days.

Back in the South, conditions had not changed. As Burns told it, attorneys took advantage of him, and prison authorities vowed to make him suffer for the bad press he had given their institutions. He spent the first few weeks as a trustee in a camp with an apparently humane warden, but once the public interest in him died down, Burns found himself transferred to a camp where conditions were just as bad as they had been years before. The pick shack (a kind of iron rack) had replaced the lash, and the sweatbox (solitary confinement in a cramped iron compartment baking in the sun) was in more general use. Prisoners still schemed to escape at any cost, and guards still seemed to derive great pleasure from unreasonably disciplining the unfortunate inmates. Burns had paid an Atlanta attorney to represent his case to the prison commission. Now the lawyer came demanding bribes for the commissioners if they were to follow through on his parole. Twice within a year the parole board set aside his appeal, ignoring the pleas of his family and the letters of support they had solicited from influential people in the Northeast and Midwest.

With hopes for parole dashed, Burns planned another escape, this time paying a farmer to have a car hidden in the woods ready to drive him to freedom. The closing chapters of the book describe this second harrowing escape and the subsequent months of hiding in various northern cities. The publication of his story was, it seemed, his last opportunity to win the sympathy of the nation and its support for his pardon.

As this summary of Burns's experiences indicates, many of the elements of human drama and pathos were present before the studio even considered an adaptation for the screen. One example is the theme of the "forgotten man," the World War I veteran who returned from Europe to face readjustment problems in the 1920s and the brunt of the Depression after 1929. This theme became commonplace in films of the 1930s, probably the most memorable illustration being in Warners' *Gold Diggers of 1933* (coincidentally another assignment of Mervyn LeRoy's), which included an entire production number based on World War I vets who were now down on their luck and looking to the government to see them through this crisis as they had seen the nation through an earlier one. In real life the vocal demands of veterans' organizations for their long overdue bonuses for wartime service, the sprouting of tent villages pointedly called Hoovervilles all across the country, and the news of thousands of unemployed veterans marching on Washington in the summer of 1932 and encamping on the Capitol Mall to demand congressional action all made the early chapters of Burns's book quite timely.

The book's criticism of complacent public officials failing to respond to flagrant injustices seemed to fit a national mood. In refusing Burns's last appeals for parole, one supposedly respectable Georgia prison commissioner had defended the chain gang system against critics in the national press. For "proof" that the chain gang did rehabilitate offenders, the commissioner used Burns himself and his rise to success during his years in Chicago as an example. But in the same breath he demanded that the prisoner serve out his full term. Clearly the state officials were more interested in protecting their outmoded institutions and their own positions within them than they were in serving justice. The images of the southern sheriff and his bureaucratic superiors became the stereotypes that persist to this day.

As noted, the book dripped with the earnestness of Burns's middle-class values. His brother's background in the clergy came through vividly too. His introduction had the unmistakable ring of a Sunday sermon. Robert had been a good, God-fearing boy who had a terrible run of bad luck; anyone with an iota of Christian charity would be able to comprehend his misfortune and be moved to speak out in his behalf. As Burns described his own personality, though, it was a strange mixture of vigorous ambition and debilitating resentfulness. He could twice apply himself to the almost impossible challenge of escaping from the chain gang and in the meanwhile achieve a degree of success in business that had to appear incredible to readers in 1932. Yet, just as naturally, he could drift along as a hobo riding the rails or blend into the anonymous underworld of the escaped fugitive. He could be audacious, ingenious, and indefatigable, but at other times he was passive and unexplainably submissive, as in the robbery and in his marriage.

Burns had described himself as a "sucker" for having gone off to war instead of staying home to look after his own career. Although some of the bonus marchers might have agreed, Burns's real reputation as a sucker should have come from his continuing feelings of responsibility toward a wife who had blackmailed him into marriage in the first place and from his willingness to return to Georgia and place his trust in the officials there when he certainly should have known better. But the attitudes that make him look a sucker—devotion to his country, loyalty to his spouse, respect for law and authority—were the very bulwarks of middle-class respectability. In a sense, therefore, the book can be seen as an unintended critique on the very values Burns was striving to espouse, and it fit in perfectly with the cynical realization of many Americans that the traditional values of previous decades might not translate well into the 1930s.

Screenwriting: Phase One

The basic elements of a successful movie plot were already present. The task at hand, then, was to put an already plotted story on the screen. The creative decisions to be made involved such questions as what scenes to add, leave out, or change in order to assist in development of the narrative; which characters to emphasize and how to portray them; how to convert Burns's first-person statements into a narrative framework that would make the same or similar points evident from an unfolding story; and how to capture the audience's attention and have them see themselves as vicariously involved.

The first writers to set themselves to these tasks were Brown Holmes and Sheridan Gibney, young men who were relatively new to the movie business. Holmes, only twenty-three years old, had grown up in California and graduated from Hollywood High School. His first screen credit had come the year before when he had worked on the script for *The Maltese Falcon*, and now he was earning seventy-five dollars a week. Gibney, only a few years older, had grown up in the East, attended a prep school, and then graduated from Amherst. He had more writing experience, having written opera librettos for a time and tried his hand at writing for the stage, but 1932 saw his first experience in Hollywood. Holmes was the first to be assigned to the project, and in mid April 1932 Hal Wallis was hurrying him to get a treatment ready within ten days so that Zanuck could look it over before he left on a trip.[4]

Of the problems that surfaced early in the screenwriting process, a few could be solved easily. The Outline, for example, had the movie ending with the main character shaking hands with another chain gang fugitive whom he quite remarkably came upon by accident on a city street corner. This seemed so unlikely as to be unbelievable (despite Burns's account of such an incident in his book). In the next version the film was to end with the fugitive's sneaking across a state line under the cover of night; in the Final script he is escaping to another country. Other problems with the early Outline and Treatment were less easily corrected, however, and several of these persisted into Gibney's Screenplay and the Holmes-Gibney Temporary script.

The most serious difficulties seemed to be in the first third of the story, which dealt with the introduction of the main character and the explanation of how he wound up in prison. It is interesting to note that from the very first, the writers were working with Paul Muni in mind for the leading role (on March 15 he had signed a contract to make four films for Warners at three thousand dollars a week), and directions were scripted in a Muni-does-this and Muni-does-that way. Holmes and Gibney went to great lengths to identify the main character (henceforth referred to as James Allen) as a war hero. While everything

4. Wallis to Holmes, April 14, 1932, Production Files, Warner Brothers Collection, University of Southern California.

suggests that Burns's military career was uneventful, Holmes's treatment opens on a battlefield, with Allen cradling a fallen comrade. Then the scene dissolves to a ceremony in which the Distinguished Service Cross is being pinned to Allen's uniform.

In this first phase of the writing, particular criticism was leveled at the powerful big businessman who was seen getting rich off the war but having no compassion for the men who had to fight it. The image was best captured in Holmes's setup for a reaction shot to the parade of returning GI's marching down a New York boulevard: "A big American flag and a big American business man lean out the window [of a skyscraper]. The Big American Businessman's paunch, grown huge on war profit, rests heavily on the window ledge. He waves his arms and cheers, and his paunch quakes with his tremendous fervor." No suggestions were offered to help the actor figure out how to present his belly in such a political way.

Two shots later, the same businessman appears behind his desk (this time "his paunch heaving heavy with satisfaction") and reneges on his promise to give Allen his old job back. "Two years is a long time," he explains, "and the man who replaced you is doing well." Callously rebuffed by the powers of big business, Allen takes to the city streets in search of a job. The scene is nicely designed around a montage of feet shuffling up and down stairs, across streets, and so forth, until his once proud army shoes are seen as scuffed and dirty with a sock showing through the sole. The disintegration of James Allen's hopes for employment and respectability is completed several shots later when he is seen trying unsuccessfully to pawn the medal he had received for valor in the war.

There were several problems here. First of all, the sharp criticism of big businessmen as unapologetic profiteers grown fat by taking advantage of the average American was probably unacceptable to studio executives. At another point in the Temporary script Holmes and Gibney were even more explicit in their critique of capitalism. Burns's book had described how he had tried panhandling to get the price of a meal. When the screenwriters incorporated that experience into the script, they included a soapbox orator praising the virtues of social democracy in the Soviet Union and collecting a nice parcel of change in his hat as he spoke: "Everyone is working—eating—living! Why? Because the country belongs to the people, that's why. Ten more years—mark my words, ladies and gentlemen—ten more years and Russia will be the greatest nation of all time." By stressing the economic and social forces opposing Allen, the Holmes-Gibney introduction to the story failed to tell enough about Allen himself. For the film to be really effective drama, the audience would have to come to emphathize with the main character in an intimate and personal way. Allen's hopes and ambitions, his fears and desires, did not come through in these early scripts.

Holmes and Gibney had more success in suggesting how the horror of prison life might be portrayed on the screen. Holmes's Treatment suggested the transition from the courtroom to the camp by having the judge's pounding of the gavel dissolve into the banging of the blacksmith's hammer that was attaching the shackles to Allen's legs. The early scripts also suggested the use of a dolly shot to introduce viewers to the bunkhouse as the house chain (a chain to which all the men are fastened) is pulled out on the first morning of Allen's stay there. They used visuals effectively to show the brutality of camp life, such as Allen having the chain thrown in his face on his first morning and Pinky (later named Red) being kicked after having collapsed from exhaustion on the rock pile. In addition, they sensed when the audience might be touched more by not seeing the action. In the bunkhouse after the first day's work, for example, the Holmes-Gibney script specified that the audience should not see Allen whipped, but should concentrate instead on the faces of the other convicts as they hear the sounds of the lash and the groans of the victim.[5]

The decision to make Allen an engineer and builder of bridges instead of a magazine publisher allowed his accomplishments to emerge impressively on the screen—a bridge taking shape could be visualized far more easily than a pile of

5. Mervyn LeRoy mistakenly takes credit for designing this scene in his autobiography (*Mervyn LeRoy: Take One*, pp. 110–11). It was clearly the work of the writers.

magazines disappearing from a newsstand. The bridge also gave them an interesting visual symbol to refer back to: Allen could propose to his girlfriend in a park overlooking a bridge, and he could pause to admire a bridge he had built, a symbol of his skill and accomplishment, as he fled the chain gang a second time (both of these scenes were eventually cut from the script). Later in the story, when the writers wanted to indicate the support that Allen had in the business community of Chicago even after his recapture in 1929, Holmes and Gibney suggested it be done visually with a scene of the chamber of commerce members Allen was supposed to have addressed cheering and applauding in support of his release. As effective as such a scene might have been, the studio decided the point could be made just as well (and a lot less expensively) by superimposing a series of newspaper headlines with the desired message.

A decade later characters in such films as *The Maltese Falcon* (the remake) might be presented as complex human beings with values and attitudes that were open to interpretation or to change. In 1932, however, Hollywood's characters still tended to be simple and unconfusing, designed to make unmistakable sense to a mass audience that had become accustomed to the broadly acted and simplified characters of the silent screen. There was no trouble identifying the villains in the work of Holmes and Gibney—the big businessman, the warden and his guards, the prison commissioners, and Allen's wife, Marie, all qualified. Still, there were some confusing contradictions and ambiguities. The wife's character was cast as twenty-six years old and sexy (Burns's actual wife, remember, was fortyish and stout), and her lines made her motives clear. A vicious and vindictive woman, she sought to dominate her husband as well as grow rich off him. She enjoyed reminding him that she knew his secret and would not hesitate to turn him in if he displeased her. Yet somehow the script suggested that she deserved sympathy too. After all, she loved Allen even if she was taking advantage of him. It was he who was unfaithful.

The other woman, Helen, was supposed to be the pure and good heroine—the beautiful person that Allen was willing to return to prison for. But her character was confused by being made a chorus girl by trade (not the usual occupation of a good girl)—a chorus girl (according to the early versions of the script) whom Allen had first seen while she was performing, of all things, a kinky chain-gang number with silver chains and a skimpy costume.

Two fellow prisoners, Bomber Wells and Barney Sykes, were partially developed as sympathetic characters. Although one was an admitted murderer serving a life sentence and the other returned to bootlegging and procuring as soon as he was released from prison, they were friendly toward Allen and helped him with advice, money, and protection during his escape. The other prisoners seemed hopeless cases. They had been totally broken by the chain gang if they weren't mental cases before they got there. Few other characters were given any personality at all in the early scripts. Allen's brother appears in passing, for example, but he takes on none of the characterization he receives in later versions of the script.

The structure and pacing of the film were at least as important as the characters, and the Holmes-Gibney Temporary script did indicate their attempts to tighten up the narrative a bit. For example, with regard to his second stint on the chain gang, a sequence dealing with Allen's short-lived term as a trustee and the stories of two other prisoners' escape attempts were left out as unnecessary. There was an eye to building suspense too, especially in dealing with Allen's first escape. Sequences dealing with the fugitive's "close shave" in a barbershop and his passing himself off as a traveling salesman when questioned by a local sheriff on his flight to the North were handled with subtlety and style. For a more exciting chase scene, events were rearranged so that Allen (instead of two black prisoners) makes his second escape in a prison truck. The story line still had some troublesome gaps, however, and some problems of continuity. For example, the Temporary script had Allen walking out of a downtown hotel and into a suburban railway station to buy a ticket with no indication of how he got from one place to the other. Also, scenes had to be added to introduce characters more smoothly. As Holmes and Gibney had it, there was no sequence dealing with Allen's renting the room from Marie. As a result, viewers would be confused about whether she was his landlady or another boarder.

Finally, Holmes and Gibney do deserve the credit for the famous closing scene in which Allen comes out of the shadows to say good-bye to Helen. Alone and afraid, convinced that the rest of his life will be spent in hiding from the law, he responds pathetically to her question, "How do you live?," with one of the best-remembered closing lines of any American film: "I steal." A shot of him sneaking across the border was supposed to follow, but the closing lines summarized perfectly the depressing conclusion that had to be drawn from the film: that a misguided and unjust social system, and a barbaric and inhumane system of law enforcement, had taken an ordinary young man who was full of the traditional and respected virtues of middle-class America and made out of him a hardened criminal.

Screenwriting: Phase Two

From the documents that are available to study the internal workings of the studio, it appears that Mervyn LeRoy had not yet been assigned to direct the film. Hal Wallis sent a copy of the Temporary script to Roy DelRuth, whose background had been in directing Mack Sennett comedies. Not surprisingly, he thought the drama was heavy and depressing. DelRuth's reply makes clear how sensitive studio people were to the whims of a mass audience ("the mob," as DelRuth called them) and how little else really concerned them. DelRuth was worried that the story was too morbid. "There is not one moment of relief anywhere," he wrote. Indicating that he realized "any attempt to inject humor into a story of this nature will injure it," he nonetheless feared that any film "of such a depressing nature" would "lack box-office appeal—especially right now, when the whole public is depressed to the extent that many of them are leaping out of windows." The last few paragraphs of his memo to Wallis were even more pointed:

> The ending of the story while unusual—is not one that the mob will like—an example of this was seen in M.G.M.'s picture "The Champ" where Berry [*sic*] died—the audience wanted him to live.

Another example was in "Hell Divers" they remade the entire ending of the picture and made it a "happy one" for box office reasons. "Two Seconds" I understand is not doing as well as expected on account of it being such a morbid and depressing affair.

The above views are merely my impressions of the story—it will probably make a good picture for Muni and he will probably be great in it but I doubt if it will ever meet with such a hearty approval from an audience, especially now that everyone has a problem of their own to solve.

I personally do not care for a story of this kind and would not like to make it.[6]

DelRuth had found the Holmes treatment "dull and drawn out," and the dialogue in the Holmes-Gibney Temporary "very ordinary." Apparently others were concerned about the project too, but Darryl Zanuck seized control of the situation.

The principals had had five weeks to review the Temporary script and react to it by the time Zanuck called his first story conference on July 7, 1932. The six pages of typed, single-spaced notes on the conference[7] provided an entirely new treatment of the beginning of the film and the development of the main character. Instead of searching for a job in the city after his return from overseas, Allen is to go directly to his hometown in New Jersey (Zanuck suggested that it be a small city of about twenty-five thousand) where his mother, his brother, and friends welcome him home. Instead of going jobless, he is welcomed back into the factory with a job better than the one he had before the war. Rather than offend the government or the business community, Zanuck has Allen's problems of adjusting to civilian life entirely psychological. As good as his job is, he finds it monotonous and unsatisfying, and he feels out of place socially. These feelings are conveyed in one scene where Allen takes his girl to a community dance and is made to feel foolish for not knowing the current steps, in another where he attends a Sunday service in his brother's church uncomfortably wearing his old uniform to please his mother, and in yet another where

6. DelRuth to Wallis, n.d., Production Files, Warner-USC.
7. Production Files, Warner-USC.

he spends his lunch hour from the factory daydreaming over the construction of a bridge nearby.

In the new treatment he confronts his family with the news that he cannot suppress the urge to become involved in building and engineering, and they reluctantly bid him well as he goes off (first to New England and later to the South and Midwest) in search of construction work. Finally, failing to find steady work, he winds up in a flophouse in an unidentified southern city and from there, as the earlier versions had it, gets involved in the holdup.

It is evident that Zanuck wanted a complete reworking of the opening part of the film, but he wanted other changes as well and the notes went on with detailed and specific suggestions. For example, they directed that as Barney shuffles up the road after his release from prison, he should hitch a ride on the wagon carrying Red's coffin. They specify how many guards should follow Allen into the bush as he escapes. They suggest that Allen try to avoid the hounds and the guards by hiding underwater and breathing through a bamboo stalk. "We can heighten the suspense and tension of this scene," Zanuck explained, "by having the dogs and men thrash around close by where he is hid [*sic*]."

If suspense was a desirable quality, so was romance, and the notes directed that the sexual element be played up in Allen's interlude with the hooker in Barney's hotel. Changes were also suggested for the text of the pro-Soviet soapbox speech, changes that the new screenwriter would find penciled into "Mr. Zanuck's copy of the script." There was a "Special Note" too, suggesting that while he was in Chicago it would seem more realistic if James Allen should change his name to Allen James. All these changes and more were prescribed, but on one matter Zanuck stood firmly behind the writers' original conception. No matter how strong Roy DelRuth and others might have felt about lightening up on the drama and grafting on some sort of happy ending, Zanuck wanted the closing scene between Allen and his girlfriend to stand the way that Holmes and Gibney had written it.

The task of seeing through all these changes and otherwise polishing and revitalizing the heretofore uneven script was given to Howard J. Green. Remembered now as the first president of the Screen Writers Guild, Green was then thirty-nine years old, and he had already enjoyed a long and productive career as a writer and producer for vaudeville. What made him a good choice for the chain gang story, however, was his experience as a news reporter in San Francisco, St. Louis, and New York. Green wrote in a matter-of-fact, realistic style, which was just what this script needed.

Within twelve days after the story conference Green had turned out a Screenplay that followed all of Zanuck's suggestions and gave the story a new sense of real-life vitality. In the process of redesigning the opening sections of the film to accord with the new treatment, Green dropped the character of the paunchy businessman and with him the idea that Allen had gotten a raw deal when he returned from the service. In Green's script Allen's old employer goes so far as to come down to the train station to join his family in welcoming the soldier home from the war, and the gesture of saving "a more important" job for the young veteran is explained with the phrase: "After all you've been through we owe you something." Zanuck's recommendation in regard to the soapbox orator was followed. Now, instead of extolling Russia, the speaker pleads for sympathy for the poor and starving people of the Far East. "We who live in the glorious land of the free," the speaker says, "must make them human beings again."

Instead of ambiguous allusions to ideological radicalism, Green's script plays up the true-to-life nature of the story. A prologue was to be inserted at the beginning of the film, a moving scroll signed by the Reverend Vincent Burns, the real fugitive's brother, which testified to the authenticity of the scenes depicting chain gang life. At several other points in the script, newspaper headlines were to be superimposed, partly to simplify and clarify a complex plot line but also to remind audiences that they had read about this story not long ago. Both of these additions, the prologue and the use of newspaper headlines, had been suggested in the story conference of July 7.

Green's script was more thorough and uncompromising in developing the major characters in the story. Marie, for example, is introduced earlier in a sequence that shows her renting a room to Allen. We see her manipulative and designing personality develop over several sequences that trace their evolving relationship. Where the earlier scripts had made her somewhat of a sympathetic character, Green paints her as all bad. She is the one who is drinking and having a wild time with other men, thus justifying Allen's relationship with Helen. Helen is no longer a chorus girl. Zanuck had suggested that Allen's romance with her be "kept on a high plane," and Green's script succeeds in presenting her as an eminently respectable and intelligent young woman.

The character of Bomber Wells is played up in these later scripts. For example, he is present in the camp that Allen is sent back to in 1929; they pick up their old friendship, and when Allen escapes the second time he takes Bomber along with him. Another character that Green played up is Allen's brother, who is given the name of Clint. He is a pompous and holier-than-thou preacher fond of spouting dogmatic platitudes and pronouncing judgments about what is best for his brother. The sermon he offers his congregation, for example, seems to be pointed especially at young James, who is having trouble readjusting to work in the shoe factory: "Now that the horrible war is over, we are all back on the field of Peace engaged in the Battle of Life. . . . Each of us fits into the scheme of things in the army of hundreds of millions. Our work may seem dull . . . trivial . . . exacting . . . but we must carry it over the top—obey our orders—respect our business generals—each a cog in a cosmic platoon that ever advances forward in the name of civilization and progress." By developing Clint as a caricature of respected establishment values, the screenwriter was making Allen's ingenuous willingness to try (within reason) to do the "right" thing seem somehow more sensible and praiseworthy. As sincere and virtuous as James Allen is, he is never the sanctimonious prig that his brother is. The central character emerges from this script as much more of a flesh-and-blood person. We get to know him so intimately in the first few minutes of the film that we are able to view the rest of the film from his point of view.

Green's script includes some interesting new ideas for visuals. One is a symbolic device that had been used widely in silent film. When the prisoners are being loaded onto the trucks for the trip to the worksite in the predawn, a team of mules is also being readied for work. Green had the scenes of the men being chained to each other and to the truck intercut with the mules being chained and harnessed. The same symbolic comparison is repeated at the end of the workday. Another ironic touch Green added was in the barbershop scene where Allen was almost captured after the first escape. The policeman who comes in and strikes up a casual conversation with the barber about the escapee happens to be thumbing through a copy of *Liberty* magazine.

Though the dramatic and gripping ending was retained, Green did inject a few notes of humor. One lighthearted moment was added in the conversation Allen has with his fellow soldiers in the ship at the very beginning of the film. When one GI who plans to go back into vaudeville with his old lion-taming act wonders out loud "if Oscar and Minnie will know me when I step back into the cage," another quips, "You better hope they do!" Another laugh comes when Allen picks up the telephone at home to find a drunk calling to find out why Marie has not shown up for her date with him. "Whatever you do," the drunk slurs, "don't tell her husband."

Finally, Green tightened the pacing of the film, especially toward the end. He cut out the montage of maps and so on that was supposed to indicate Allen's travel after his second escape, and he cut the scene that had the fugitive stop for a moment to admire one of the bridges he himself had helped to build. Instead, Green heightened the excitement of the second escape by having Bomber throw sticks of dynamite at the pursuing cars until he is shot and killed. Then he added a violent and dramatic twist. Allen blows up a bridge (rather than admiring it) in order to ensure his success in fleeing from the prison guards. The story then turns directly to his meeting with Helen and the powerful closing line. The destruction of the bridge was the visual equivalent of the words "I steal" because it too indicated to what extent the system had twisted and destroyed Allen's values and his outlook on life.

Once Green's revision was ready, a second story conference took place. This time the comments were fewer and the typewritten notes ran to only a page and a half, but they illustrate again the very close attention that the executives were paying to the writer's work.[8] The most interesting specific suggestions involved the character of Allen, who at times appeared too much the "good boy," and a few points in the dialogue that were criticized as "too poetic."

The Final shooting script was ready on July 23, none too early, for production had been scheduled to begin on July 28. It concentrated on polishing up the dialogue and tightening the narrative so that some scenes in the long and rambling story might be cut. Among the scenes deleted were Clint's sermon, Allen's attempt to reenlist in the service before he got into trouble (he was to have been turned down for flat feet), and his impersonation of a traveling salesman to escape detection while fleeing from the South. Some of the scenes in the camp, especially during Allen's second confinement, were cut as well, and in the process several specific details of prison camp life (the sweatbox and pick shack, for example) went with them. Doing so had the effect of watering down to some extent the effectiveness of the film as an exposé, although any such intention is unlikely.

A few last-minute changes were even made on the first day of shooting, July 28. These involved still more economizing by cutting additional scenes. The hometown dance scene was deleted, and the character of Allen's hometown girlfriend was reduced to almost nothing. The best line in the dance scene was saved, however (a comment about how Allen had looked so much more distinguished in his uniform), and simply shifted to the homecoming at the railroad station. The hometown gal would

8. N.d., Production Files, Warner-USC.

never be missed. With Linda the hooker, Marie the wife, and Helen the true love, there were already enough women in Allen's life.

This then was the 143-page manuscript presented to Mervyn LeRoy and his production crew.

Production

Researchers today can be thankful that the production of a film also produced a lot of paper. Records of the studio's activities provide valuable insights into daily routine of the moviemaking business. Even when they lead to no great revelations, such pieces of documentary evidence allow us to understand better some procedures that before we could only guess about. For example, the Daily Production and Progress Report forms, which had to be completed at the end of each day of shooting, were carefully designed to keep a director's eye on the clock and on the budget. The forms required that a listing be made of all cast members being paid for the day with an indication of whether they worked or were "held over." In these early days of sound they called for a separate listing of the "Vitaphone Staff" and the "Picture Staff." They specified the exact time devoted to work each day and the hours set aside for lunch and dinner. They detailed the locations of the filming, the extra equipment used (buses to move from one location to another, for example), the scenes shot, the number of takes per scene, whether a take was ruined because of an actor's error or some other reason, and the time each scene took to rehearse and get on film. As a pointed reminder to the director, each day's form had to specify the number of days he had been working on the project, when he was supposed to be finished, the number of scenes remaining to be shot, and how much of the film he was expected to complete each working day.

The daily reports for *Chain Gang* indicate that Mervyn LeRoy was supposed to shoot an average of thirteen and a half scenes per day and finish the film in one month.[9] The schedule had been carefully arranged to make most economical use of the

9. Production Files, Warner-USC.

talent, most of whom were hired by the day or week and had to be paid whether they worked or not. The first two days of shooting, for example, concentrated on the scenes in the flophouse, the holdup in the diner, and the sentencing in the courtroom, so that Preston Foster and Berton Churchill, who played the robber and the judge, could finish their roles and get on to other projects. Then they proceeded to filming three days of prison camp interiors on Stage 8 at the studio. The following morning cast and crew boarded three buses, which carried them to the studio's "ranch" in the hills for exterior shooting. For almost six weeks (six days a week and two Sundays as well) they put in ten, twelve, and fourteen hours a day working at either the ranch or one or another sound stage. Thanks to process shots and rear projection effects created on the set, only two location shots required them to leave studio property—one at a nearby rock quarry and another at a Pasadena railroad station. The blowing up of the bridge at the end of Allen's exciting second escape was filmed in miniature. By and large, although the shooting schedule went on a few days longer than expected (until September 7), the filming went smoothly. The only specific delay noted in the daily summaries was a wait of several hours to allow the murky water to clear in the tank used for underwater photography. While LeRoy usually managed to easily surpass his goal of thirteen and a half scenes per day, most of the delay in the shooting schedule was due to his filming of 277 "added scenes" (in addition to the 354 scripted for the film) to provide different camera angles and slightly altered versions of the action for the people in the cutting department to choose from in constructing the final film.

The *Chain Gang* papers include cost breakdowns that show the portions of the overall production cost of $195,845 devoted to writers, director, actors, cameramen, set construction, property rental, film stock, developing, and printing. In most cases the salaries were computed as a prorated weekly payment against the employees' annual contract. For example, director LeRoy devoted eight weeks to the project at his standard $1,650 a week, while Sol Polito, the head cameraman, got $400 for each of his six weeks of work. Paul Muni was the only actor who was paid "for the part"—he got $16,750. In comparison, Noel Francis earned $100 for one day's work playing the role of Linda. The cost of building the sets is detailed with separate figures for the construction crews, electricians, "property labor," and "extra talent." By far the most expensive sets were the prison blacksmith shop ($4,895) and mess hall ($3,300). The total cost of sets (including the calendars and maps, the blowing up of the miniature bridge, and other trick shots) came to $44,830.[10] Finally, the studio production files also include various memos that offer tantalizing tidbits of information. One of them set the "final definite title on the Fugitive picture," but gave no hint as to what alternatives they might have considered.[11]

The two most important personalities in the production phase of the film were Paul Muni and Mervyn LeRoy. Muni's preparation for the role included extensive experience on the New York stage dating back to his childhood in the Yiddish theater. In fact, he had to take a six-week leave from his current Broadway hit, *Counselor-at-Law*, to make the movie in Hollywood. The reviewers were unanimous in their praise for Muni's performance in the film, and it is clear that without his commanding presence on the screen the film could not have worn as well as it has over the past half century.[12]

Director Mervyn LeRoy certainly deserves credit for coaxing the best out of Muni and for his obvious craftsmanship in bringing the screenplay to life. He was hampered, however, by a script that called for strictly two-dimensional characters. One wishes that he had overcome that handicap and made the portrayals more human and more real, but he did not. The prison guards remained uniformly callous and unfeeling, and the prostitute was a seductress and nothing more (unlike the more sensi-

10. These data are from the Weekly Production Cost Summaries, Production Files, Warner-USC.

11. Zanuck to All Department Heads, September 6, 1932, Production Files, Warner-USC.

12. See, for example, reviews in *New York Times*, November 11, 1932, and *Variety*, November 15, 1932. On Muni see Jerome Lawrence, *Actor: The Life and Times of Paul Muni* (New York: Putnam, 1974).

tive role she played in the book). The role of Allen's mother was played as written, a simple, patient, devoted woman—a saint. Perhaps the most memorable of these stereotyped characters is Allen's brother, an unrelievedly saccharine, holier-than-thou preacher. The real Reverend Mr. Burns was so dismayed with the portrayal that he brought suit against the studio for $250,000 alleging that he was "falsely and maliciously" impersonated in the film "in the character of a weak, repulsive, and hypocritical being."[13]

Although LeRoy did what his job required—directing the actors' lines and camera movements and supervising the construction of sets, the lighting, and other technical elements that effectively re-created the dank and eerie atmosphere of the prison camps on the screen—there must be some question about how influential he was in shaping the movie. For example, many of the most convincing (and Academy Award–winning) sound effects in the film were added later in the editing process, which was typically overseen by producer Zanuck. There is no evidence that LeRoy had anything to say about such decisions. Unlike some other directors (John Ford, for example) who are said to have "edited in the camera" by providing the post-production people with few alternatives to choose from, LeRoy shot 277 more scenes than the script actually called for. Working under Zanuck's watchful eye, the people in the cutting department succeeded in deleting more unnecessary scenes, rearranging a few others, and heightening the pace of the film, especially around the two escape scenes (see Notes to the Screenplay).

The daily summaries enable us to document what was shot and compare it with what got into the film. As an example, on August 30 LeRoy filmed three different versions of scene 354 in the script, the shot that was to follow Allen's last dramatic meeting with Helen and show him fleeing to safety across the border. These three versions went to the editing room, but none of them made it to the screen. Sometime between September 7 (when the shooting was finished) and October 14 (when the completed movie was previewed for selected reviewers and studio person-

13. *Newark Evening News*, February 12, 1935.

nel) the decision was made to delete this closing scene and let the final fade come as Allen retreats into the shadows, echoing the tragic "I steal." All this clearly contradicts the casual statements of critics and commentators since 1932 who almost always praise LeRoy himself for the film's haunting conclusion. In his autobiography LeRoy not only took credit for the ending as it appeared on the screen, but claimed that the idea for having Muni disappear into the shadows had come to him accidentally when a fuse blew, plunging the set into blackness.[14] In fact, the retreat into the darkness was specifically called for in the script. Taken together then, the daily summary sheets, the memos, the versions of the script, the conference notes, and the other documentary evidence support Zanuck's contention (made in an interview almost forty years later) that he deserved more of the creative credit for this film than LeRoy did.[15]

Reception and Aftermath

Variety's reviewer was less than enthusiastic about the studio preview of *Chain Gang*. Not unexpectedly, in such a trade-oriented publication his main concerns were commercial. "Tied up with the current chain gang abolition activity, it may draw attention," he observed in his review of October 22, 1932, "but its chances of getting into the important money are slim." The reviewer thought that the film would "not hold entertainment for the women or younger people" and noted that the "revolting" scenes of "the supposed atrocities" in the prison camps had caused "a great number of walkouts" at the preview. An interoffice memo suggests that the studio salespeople had been concerned too. But *Variety* and Warners' sales department were wrong. A cable Zanuck received from New York soon after the movie opened reported the film to be a smashing success and carried congratulations from "the entire sales department" to Zanuck and his production staff. We "must admit," the telegram continued, "you people were right when we asked you to

14. LeRoy, *Mervyn LeRoy: Take One*, p. 110.
15. Mel Gussow, *Don't Say Yes until I Finish Talking: A Biography of Darryl F. Zanuck* (New York: Doubleday, 1971), p. 48.

cut down on blood and brutal sequences and you refused." The cable concluded: "Audiences throughout America have vindicated your decision." Another telegram brought exciting news about opening night in New York: "FUGITIVE BIGGEST BROADWAY SENSATION IN LAST THREE YEARS STOP THOUSANDS TURNED AWAY FROM BOX OFFICE TONIGHT WITH LOBBY DELAY HELD FOUR HOURS STOP . . . CAN'T REFRAIN FROM WIRING YOU TONIGHT AS WARNER PROSPERITY TURNS CORNER IN TWO HUNDRED NINE OTHER CITIES WHERE FUGITIVE OPENED."[16]

At least some of the film's success was due to an all-out publicity campaign to help theater operators attract an audience. Anticipating the problems noted by the *Variety* reviewer, several of the elements of that campaign were designed specifically to appeal to women. Although very little screen time was devoted to Burns's love life, the story was played up as a mixture of "sweet romance and grim drama." A fashion feature for the women's page with pictures of the female stars decked out in current styles was provided for use by local newspapers, and a tie-up was suggested with the sale of a specially designed "Glenda Farrell gown" at local department stores. Special posters were laid out to emphasize in a suggestive way the role of women in the fugitive's life, and for those potential moviegoers interested in social psychology, one press book story stressed the influence of women on the criminal mind: "Find the woman—and you will find the actual driving force behind the criminal mentality as has been proven in hundreds of case histories. Dr. Hugo Goritz, eminent criminologist of Vienna, states that the woman is at the root of the crime in ninety-seven cases out of a hundred. And, states Dr. Goritz, this woman is usually a blonde. Pictured above is Glenda Farrell, motion picture temptress, as the personification of the 'moll,' in 'I Am a Fugitive from a Chain Gang.'" Here is an interesting example of the insights film history can add to our understanding of social val-

16. The cable from MICALOVE in New York to Zanuck was quoted in an interoffice memo from Zanuck to All Writers, Directors, Supervisors and Department Heads, November 11, 1932. The second cable was from Charlie Enfield, both from Production Files, Warner-USC.

ues.[17] That the publicity department at a major Hollywood studio, supposed experts at predicting the public's response to such stimuli, should think this to be an appropriate observation to evoke interest and support says a great deal about perceived attitudes toward American women at that time.

Typically the press material for a Hollywood film contained pap stories that reviewers might be expected to use to spice up their comments about the movie and standard press releases and advertisements that the exhibitor was invited to place in his local newspapers. In the case of *Chain Gang* these stories played up the "authenticity" of the film with displays of reprinted headlines on Burns's actual story. They boasted of having recruited two special consultants—one a former prisoner and the other a former chain gang guard—to help design the prison camp sets. They made much of the fact that the real fugitive had himself traveled across the country to assist the writers in transforming his book into a screenplay. As the story had it, Burns was only in California for a few days when he got nervous that the authorities might be on his trail and disappeared. There was also a cute story of how Paul Muni, while wearing his prison stripes on his way to work one morning, had been stopped and questioned by a rookie Los Angeles motorcycle cop. For reprinting in local papers the studio provided an illustrated six-part "fictionalization" of the story and printed dozens of ads with the copy for each more exaggerated than the last: "At Last the Truth on Chain Gang Prison Camps. . . . Every Anguished Bloodstained Word Is True. . . . Thousands suffered the tortures of the damned that it might be made. Now here is the authentic truth about a present day hell-on-earth, written in blood by a convict who is still in flight from the horrors he dared expose." In this case the hyperbole of the ad copy was matched by the garish illustrations of "medieval type" torture devices, which inevitably played upon the audience's unconscious fantasies.

Although Burns had been paid outright for his rights to his

17. For additional comment on the film's portrayal of women see Russell Campbell, "I Am a Fugitive from a Chain Gang," *Velvet Light Trap*, June 1971, pp. 17–20.

story and had nothing financial to gain, he did risk capture by publicizing the film in the New York area. The fugitive had found friends in high places. New Jersey Governor A. Harry Moore had met with him secretly in the summer of 1932 and informally agreed to favor him in an extradition hearing if one became necessary. Emboldened by such indications of support and by the passage of time, Burns began to take some chances. A week or so before the film was to open, he traveled to New York and dropped in unexpectedly on Paul Muni in the dressing room of the Broadway theater in which he was then appearing. Burns also allowed the studio publicists to arrange a meeting and interview with several of the New York newspaper reviewers, who were carefully blindfolded before being driven across the river to his New Jersey hideout.[18]

After the movie opened on November 9, Burns seemed to have lost his head completely. He made public appearances in Trenton and Plainfield to publicize the movie, and he allowed himself to be interviewed at length by a reporter from the *Newark Sunday Call.* The *Call* story said that Burns had come to Newark two years before, after fleeing from Georgia the second time, and had lived in the area ever since. Although it was meant to be a sympathetic retelling of the fugitive's story, the article made the police look foolish by telling how this "wanted man" had been able to travel around the state with impunity. Worse still, it provided the authorities with a virtual roadmap by which to find him. It indicated that he was living in East Orange, a Newark suburb, and explained that his hair had grayed somewhat over the past two years and that now he wore glasses; just to be sure there was no mistake, it included a recent picture of him. Three days later the Newark police, armed with warrants from Georgia, arrested Burns again. The newspaper stories of the arrest suggest that the local authorities may have been moved to action in Burns's case to divert public attention from a nagging scandal involving some misplaced ballots from the November election.[19]

18. *New York Herald Tribune*, November 27, 1932.

19. *Newark Sunday Call*, December 11, 1932; *Newark Evening News*, December 18, 1932.

For the next ten days there was again a wave of free press for the movie as Burns was held in a Newark jail pending a hearing before the governor on his extradition. When the hearing was held on December 21, Governor Moore ignored the representations of an assistant attorney general sent up from Georgia and freed the prisoner with an injunction that he live the life of a decent citizen and avoid further publicity.[20] It was good advice, but Burns could not keep his name out of the papers for long. Fourteen months later he was trying out a vaudeville act in which he and a quartet of black ex-convicts sang songs about the chain gang, "revealing details of prison life not shown in the movie."[21]

Eventually Robert Burns's story did have a happy ending. For thirteen years following the production of the film there were renewed attempts by the Georgia authorities to bring back the fugitive, but three successive New Jersey governors refused to extradite him. Burns's poor old mother, tortured through all of her son's ordeal, sent Jack Warner a pathetic handwritten note at one point in the struggle asking the studio chief to send more letters of support.[22] Eventually, in 1945, Burns returned to the South, this time at the personal invitation of Georgia Governor

20. *Newark Evening News*, December 22, 1932.

21. *Newark Evening News*, February 2, 1934. Perhaps his instinct for publicity ran in the family, for in the mid 1930s Burns's brother also earned his share of notoriety. In February 1935, as the famous trial of Bruno Hauptmann for kidnapping and murdering the infant son of Charles Lindbergh was drawing to a close, a crazed minister jumped up on a windowsill and screamed out that someone else had confessed to the crime in his Fort Lee, New Jersey, church. The minister, who barely escaped being charged with contempt and was pictured on several front pages being escorted from the courtroom by two burly state troopers, was none other than Vincent Burns. Over the next few years he won a flurry of news stories for being deprived of his pulpit and locked out of his church by an irate congregation and later for a series of court appearances concerning his refusal to pay $14.70 in charges for overtime telephone calls. As his wife put it in her 1936 suit for divorce, after helping his brother prepare the chain gang book and seeing the story made into a film he had become "unbearably vainglorious" and "an indefensible slave to an ever expanding desire for publicity." See clipping file, Newark Public Library.

22. Mrs. Burns to Warner, August 28, 1937, Legal Files, Warner Brothers Collection, Princeton University.

Ellis Arnall, who personally pled his case before the prison commission and won the fugitive a commutation of his life sentence and release from all obligations to that state.[23] Finally he had become a free man.

Until his death in 1955 Robert E. Burns lived in a suburb in New Jersey, supporting himself as a tax consultant. Except for a few vain thoughts of turning his chain gang story into a television series,[24] he seemed to forget the turbulent years of his life outside the law. Brother Vincent was less successful in finding peace within himself. As late as 1956 he was still suing the estate of his brother for fifty thousand dollars he claimed to be due him as a share in the royalties from the original chain gang book.[25]

To what extent did *I Am a Fugitive from a Chain Gang* represent an effort by Warner Brothers studio to exercise its talents for social reform? Interviewed for *Silver Screen* magazine, Paul Muni was quoted as saying: "I would be something less than human not to have seized the chance to expose such evil in *I Am a Fugitive.* Of course," Muni went on, "I am an actor, not a reformer, nor a psychologist, nor anything of the sort. Just a player of parts. But, nevertheless, the theater has from time to time accomplished wonders for mankind. And the screen with its unlimited appeal, is a vastly more far reaching medium. Hollywood, if it will, can arouse the world against all sorts of evils."[26]

If the intent of the studio had been to mount a social crusade of some sort, one logical place to find evidence for it would be in the publicity campaign. As noted, the press package stressed the veracity of the story and the brutality suffered by the central character, and it included garish displays of chains and whipping posts and associated them with "medieval practices." In addition, it tied in the recent Florida case of two prison camp guards who were tried for the murder of an inmate who died in one of the infamous sweatboxes. "What a picture to do things with," the press book exclaimed. "If you get behind" the pic-

23. *Newark Evening News*, November 1, 2, and 3, 1945.

24. Burns to Warner, September 4, 1951, Legal Files, Warner-Princeton.

25. *Newark Evening News*, October 25, 1956.

26. "Champion of the Underdog," *Silver Screen*, December 1932.

ture, exhibitors were told, "you can tear the town wide open—have editors writing editorials about it—have priests, ministers and rabbis shouting about it from the pulpits—and have the public storming your doors to see it." Invariably what such reviewers wrote and clergymen preached turned out to be appeals for prison reform, but the studio press material tried to be objective about the actual politics of the situation, as illustrated by the questions suggested to be asked by the local newspapers' "inquiring reporter." One read: "Do you think the chain gang system should be abolished by federal law if the states refuse to abandon it?" But another asked: "Do you believe the chain gang penal system would decrease crime if adopted in this state?"

The response of many reviewers was to spice their comments on the movie with editorializing about the need for prison reform. Their writing may have influenced contemporary audiences and subsequent critics to see the film as even more of a social document than the producers intended. Louella Parsons's review in the *Los Angeles Examiner* proclaimed that, although she was "usually a conscientious objector when it comes to motion pictures that are propaganda in any form," she found *Chain Gang* to be "a glorious exception." She went on to conclude that "if this motion picture . . . can do anything to correct an evil that is a blot on civilization, it will not have been made in vain." *Motion Picture Herald* for December 3, 1932, quoted an editorial written for the Hearst chain of newspapers in praise of the film: although "effective protest against social injustice and cruelty has been made in printed books," Arthur Brisbane argued, "the moving picture more powerfully and effectively than any other agency will work against brutality, by actually enabling millions to SEE IT, instead of merely reading it. What men see, with their own eyes, or the eye of the camera, influences them most powerfully." Commenting specifically on *Chain Gang*, Brisbane went on: "You should see this picture [and] advise other men to see it, and thus help to arouse public opinion against a shameful prison system."

Another external factor that may have influenced people to think of the film as a crusading document was the publicity given to a series of suits brought against the moviemakers by

Georgia prison officials who (unswayed by the fact that the film had carefully avoided identifying their state) thought their reputations had been unjustly smeared.[27] What got less treatment in the papers was the studio's decision to pay off the plaintiffs rather than persist in a defense of the truthfulness of their film. Such a legal campaign might have had a real impact on public and political opinion, but it also would have cost a lot of money.

Although many of the studio people had agreed with Roy DelRuth that it was a mistake to make the chain gang picture because the very real social issues portrayed might decrease its entertainment value, Zanuck had disagreed and stuck with the project, believing that the excitement inherent in the story could make up for whatever else it may have lacked. If special care were taken in screenwriting and publicity, he thought, the controversial and realistic quality of the film could be retained without limiting the potential audience. After all, it was not as if Zanuck and his movie were on the cutting edge of a movement for radical reform. Revelations about the chain gang system had been common in the popular literature of the 1920s, and journals of liberal opinion commented on the problem regularly. The film did not expose anything that had not been written about over and over again. As noted, in the process of tightening the script, references to some of the most inhumane prison camp practices had been deleted. Moreover, as several reviewers noted, the film missed the opportunity to examine critically very important aspects of the problem. There was no attempt, for example, to understand the psychology of the brutal guards. Pare Lorentz, writing in *Vanity Fair*, thought the film might have been far more effective if the producers had, "like the Germans and the Russians at their best," used the story and the characters as a vehicle for "making the prison, and not the actors, the object of the film."[28] Zanuck had faith enough in the story and his own sense of the public's taste to induce the studio to risk a film project that did not fit the typical Hollywood formula. It should not be sur-

27. See clipping file at Academy of Motion Picture Arts and Sciences, Beverly Hills, and New York Public Library.

28. Pare Lorentz, *Lorentz on Film: Movies 1927 to 1941* (New York: Hopkinson and Blake, 1975), p. 99.

prising that when conflicts arose—whether they were of a dramatic, a commercial, or ideological nature—the potential power of the social drama was compromised.

In noting where and why the film pulled its punches, however, we should not underestimate *I Am a Fugitive from a Chain Gang* as a forceful social document. There can be no doubt that, although liberals and intellectuals had known about the problem for years, the experience of seeing this film awakened millions of American people to an issue and helped to create the political climate in which real reform could eventually take place. The producers had restrained the writing staff from designing a film more critical of the capitalist system, but the movie did satirize such bastions of middle-class respectability as the businessman (Burns's employer at the shoe factory) and the local clergyman. More pointedly, it showed Depression audiences another example of the traditional American success story by tracing Allen's rise in the engineering profession and the Chicago business community. But this time there was no happy ending. James Allen's hopes were dashed, by the same type of overwhelming social forces that threatened the lives of average and ordinary Americans in 1932. As this film and the other Warner Brothers films of social consciousness showed, movies could be commercially successful even if they did address real social problems. As Darryl Zanuck seemed to know from the beginning, the secret was to make them well.

I am grateful to the following archivists, who helped me in the course of this project: Robert Knudtsen, Special Collections, Research Library, University of Southern California; Mary Ann Jensen, Theatre Collection, Princeton University Library; Charles F. Cummings, New Jersey Reference Division, Newark Public Library, Newark, New Jersey.

1. *Returning from France on the troop transport, Sergeant James Allen joins his buddies in sharing dreams for the future.*

2. *Allen tries to explain to his mother why he does not want to go back to his old job at the shoe factory.*

3. Clint is the portrait of a sanctimonious preacher when he urges Allen to return to work as "a soldier of peace instead of a soldier of war."

4. Mr. Parker assures Allen that he will easily readjust to the factory. "Before you know it, you'll be doing it again with your eyes shut."

5. *Allen gets news of his layoff from his first construction job.*

6. *When he tries to pawn his war medal Allen learns that there is a glut on the market.*

7. *With a shocked expression Allen realizes that he has been tricked into taking part in a holdup.*

8. *The police corner Allen outside the diner.*

9. *As the convicts trudge off to the morning meal this low-angle shot accentuates the chains dragging to the floor.*

10. *At the breakfast table Bomber Wells (right) and Barney Sykes (left) are introduced in an eye-level shot that encourages viewers to think of themselves as fellow prisoners.*

11. *The team of mules is being harnessed for the day's work, just as the men are.*

12. *At the quarry Allen gets his first taste of forced labor.*

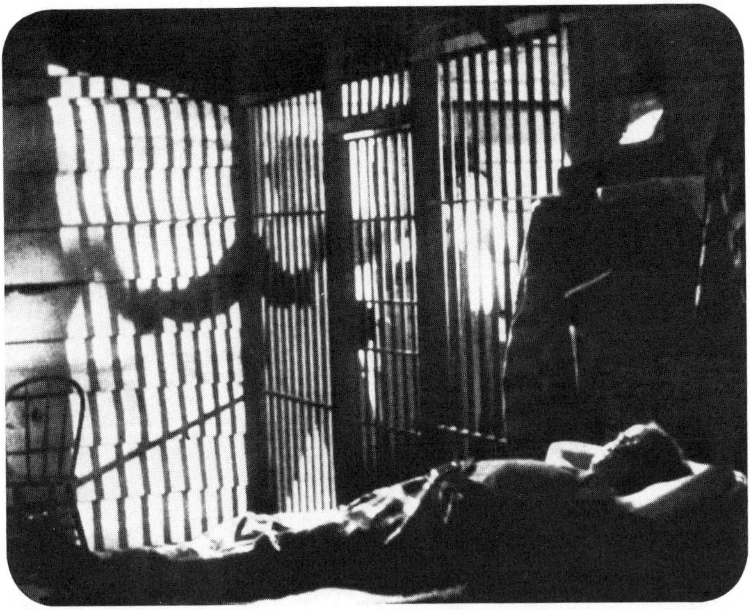

13. *Viewers hear the lash but see only shadows as Allen is whipped at the end of his first day on the chain gang.*

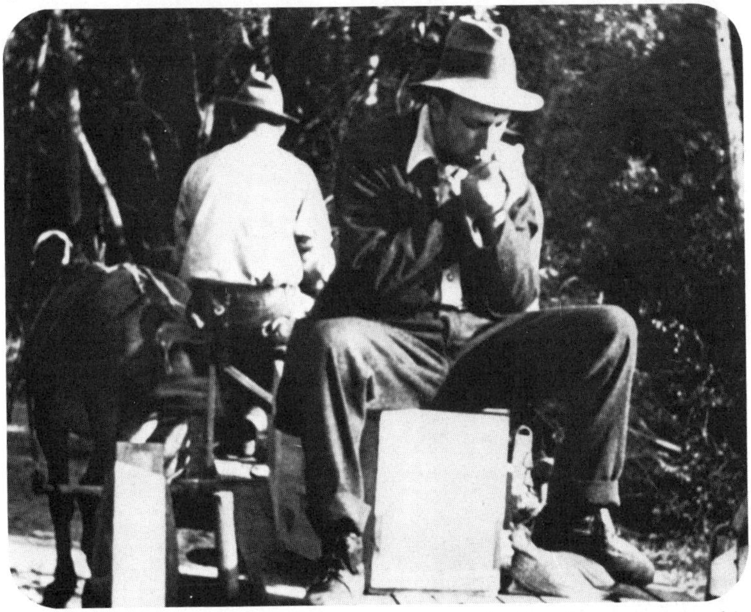

14. *Hitching a ride into town, Barney sits atop Red's coffin and strikes his match against it.*

15. *Allen asks Sebastian to bend his shackles. This scene and the whipping scene (figure 13) are mocked in Woody Allen's* Take the Money and Run.

16. *On the run, Allen hides underwater, breathing through a reed as one of the pursuing guards thrashes about nearby.*

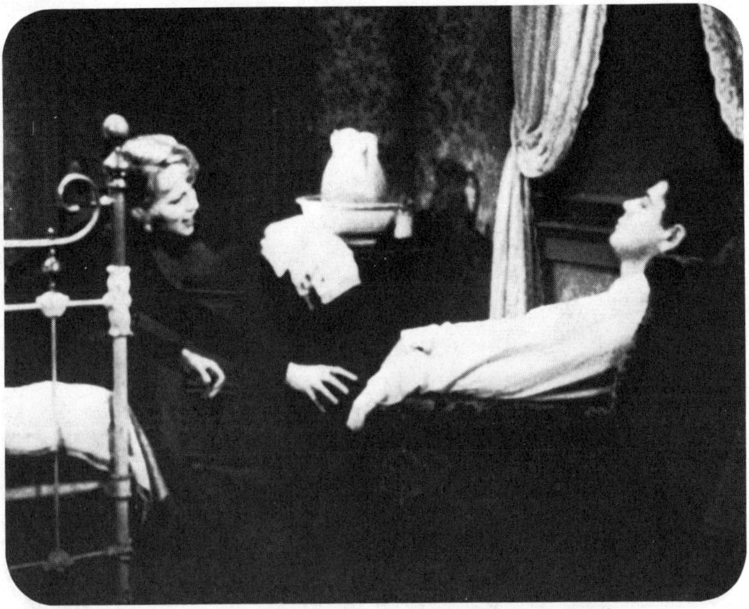

17. *Linda, the good-hearted prostitute, touches Allen's leg and offers: "If there's anything I can do to help you, just say the word."*

18. *Allen cowers in the doorway of the train as the sheriff's men chase a hobo they believe to be him.*

19. *Marie schemes to blackmail Allen into marriage by threatening to tell his secret.*

20. *Allen, now risen to general field superintendent, and one of his assistants admire a model of one of their latest bridge-building projects.*

21. *At the Club Chateau, Allen meets Helen and begins to fall in love.*

Want Him Back!
JAMES ALLEN BLOCK
JUSTICE IN ILLINOIS
Chicago officials have refused to grant extr
dition in the case of James Allen, desperate
convict who escaped from a chain gang in th
state a few years ago.
Local officials will make every effort to
their demands that Allen be returned to this
to complete his sentence.
Allen's escape was one of the most
in the history of prison camps,
for months after he fled from
good his escape.
The action of the Chicago

22. *Inserts of newspapers are used to visualize the controversy over Allen's struggle to avoid extradition.*

23. *"Swing 'em high . . . !" Back at the chain gang, sledges swing in perfect synchronization to a "Negro song."*

24. *The prison commission denies Allen's plea for a pardon.*

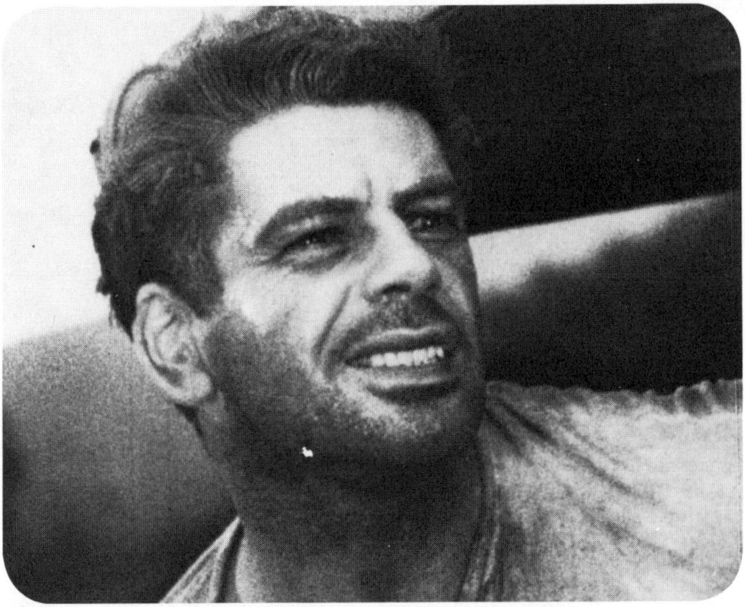

25. *During his final escape Allen "watches tensely" as the bridge he dynamited blows up.*

26. *Months later, Allen meets Helen for one last time. Then he retreats into the shadows and the film ends.*

I Am a Fugitive from a Chain Gang

Screenplay

by

HOWARD J. GREEN

BROWN HOLMES

and

SHERIDAN GIBNEY

I Am a Fugitive from a Chain Gang

FADE IN ON:

THE FOREWORD

It unfolds itself in a moving scroll.[1] Its text is as follows:

FOREWORD

My brother, Robert E. Burns, is now a fugitive from a chain gang. . . .

He has been branded a convict—and that makes him a hunted thing on the earth . . .

The scenes in "I Am a Fugitive" which depict life in a chain gang are true and authentic, being based upon my brother's experiences.

Rev. Vincent G. Burns
Church
Palisades, New Jersey

FADE OUT

FADE IN

1. STOCK SHOT

An American transport is plowing through water. Her deck is swarmed with soldiers in the uniform of the A.E.F.

The front page of a New York newspaper superimposes itself over this shot. A large-lettered headline reads:

SUNSET DIVISION RETURNING HOME TODAY

DISSOLVE TO:

2. INT. HOLD OF TRANSPORT

The bunks are lined three deep and are crowded very close together.[2] Most of the soldiers who are down in the hold are shooting craps in a noisy game that occupies the center of the floor. Several soldiers sit with their feet dangling from the upper bunks, watching the game. Still others are in their bunks, resting or reading. Another sits on the edge of the bunk blowing his lungs out on a harmonica; what he plays is a sour, unharmonious rendition of "There Are Smiles." Other soldiers are singing along with it.

Bringing our camera closer to the crap game we find a heterogeneous bunch of privates in the Engineering Corps—a cross-section of American youth from all stations of life—oblivious of everything except the rolling of the bones. There are probably a dozen in the crap game. They are all talking at once as they excitedly participate in the game.

There is a pile of money in the center of the ring as a colored boy excitedly lets the bones roll, his eyes bulging and his fingers snapping. Evidently he makes his point, for he takes in the money with a big grin.

COLORED BOY:

Hot diggity!

He quickly counts the money to himself.

3. CLOSE-UP

of Sergeant James Allen as he climbs down the hatchway. His feet come into the shot first. We get a good look at him as he turns around when he reaches the deck. He looks toward the crap shooters. Allen is a regular fellow not obsessed with the importance of what his chevron signifies.

ALLEN:

Sorry to break up the game, boys—the old man's having bunk inspection in an hour.

4. LONGER SHOT

as the bunch of crap shooters groan with disgust and make ad lib remarks.[3]

SECOND PRIVATE (above the din of ad libs):
Bunk is right!

The colored boy picks up the money with a grin and shuffles off-scene, counting his winnings. The other fellows go sulkily to their bunks to prepare for inspection, and throughout the rest of the scene they are getting ready, busily tidying up their bunks, cleaning rifles, and attending to other preinspection chores.

Allen stands leaning against one of the bunks while they make their inspection preparation.

5. GROUP SHOT
of the group near Allen. They include a Texan, the first private, Steve, and a couple of other soldiers. Allen is also in this shot.

TEXAN (with an unmistakable southwestern drawl):
This man's army is one inspection after another—but when I get back on that Texas range, the first man who says "inspection" to me will be S.O.L. . . . he'll hear right from my six-shooter.

FIRST PRIVATE (with a happy grin):
There'll be no inspection where *I'm* going.

ALLEN:
Where's that?

FIRST PRIVATE:
Back into vaudeville—with my old lion-taming act . . . (Looking dreamily into space.) I wonder if Oscar and Minnie will know me when I step back into the cage.

TEXAN (to first private):
You better hope they do!

FIRST PRIVATE (thinking of Oscar and Minnie and ignoring the interruption):
Gee, that'll be a thrill! And what a rest it's going to be—after this merry-go-round!

The rest laugh.

ALLEN (to Steve):
What are your plans, Steve?

STEVE:
I dunno. I had a saloon in Omaha—but they closed it up on me while I was over here— (Disgustedly.) Prohibition!

ALLEN:
That won't last long . . .

STEVE (worried):
I guess not—but I wish I knew what I was gonna do.

ALLEN:
Why don't you do like me—look for some kind of a construction job?[4]

STEVE:
I didn't know that was your line, Sergeant.

ALLEN (with a seriousness):
It wasn't—but it's going to be . . . I've been reading up on engineering—studying it every chance I get—and being in the Engineering Corps has been swell experience.[5]

FIRST PRIVATE:
We'll be reading about you in the newspapers I bet: "Mr. James Allen is building a new Panama Canal," or something.

6. CLOSE-UP
of Allen. He is set in his new ambition.

ALLEN (determined):
One thing you *can* bet: Mr. James Allen isn't going back to the old grind of a factory . . .[6]

DISSOLVE INTO:

7. STOCK SHOT

Returning soldiers marching down Broadway. Crowds line the streets and lean out of office windows, cheering, showering paper, waving flags as they welcome the returned heroes.

8. MED. SHOT

as lines of soldiers march past. Among them, close to the camera, is Sergeant James Allen. The roaring welcome of the crowd comes over the scene.[7]

DISSOLVE INTO:

9. CLOSE SHOT

of moving train wheels. We hear an engine whistle.

DISSOLVE INTO:

10. EXT. HOMETOWN STATION LONG SHOT

of scattered groups of townspeople waiting for the train to come in. The train is pulling into the station.[8]

11. CLOSER SHOT

of the group waiting for Allen. It includes his mother, his brother (dressed in ministerial garb), his hometown gal, his employer, and several other friends.[9] They are all in the foreground. In the background the train is seen as it slows down to come to a stop.

ALICE (she is the hometown gal; she gushes to Allen's mother):

Aren't you *excited*, Mrs. Allen? *I* am!

MOTHER (with a happy smile):

I've been waiting for this moment ever since my boy put on his uniform . . . I wonder if he'll be wearing his medal!

ALICE:

Sure he will![10]

The brother and the other men have been looking toward the train as if to get a glimpse of Allen.

BROTHER:

Come on, Mother . . .

They all start off in one direction.

12. LONGER SHOT

as they look along the rear coaches for a sight of the returned hero.

13. CLOSE-UP

of Allen with his kit bag. He wears civilian clothes, evidently brand new. He has alighted from a front coach and is looking for his folks. Evidently he spies them. His face lights happily. He hurries in their direction.

14. MED. SHOT

Allen's "welcome home" party all stand with their backs toward him, looking at the rear coaches as Allen comes up. His spirits are high and he is glad to be home. He is joyous at seeing his mother. He drops his kit bag as he gets an idea to surprise her. He suddenly puts his hands over her eyes and gives her a quick kiss on the back of her neck.

ALLEN:

Guess who?

They all turn at the sound of his voice.

MOTHER (as she clasps him in her arms):

Jim!

ALLEN:

Mother!

They remain in embrace while the rest look on, happy. Allen's mother now gives him a typical appraisal.

MOTHER:

You're a little thinner, Jim.

ALLEN:

Think so? Well—your cooking will fix me up.

Something about Jim puzzles her. Now she knows what it is.

MOTHER (just a little disappointed and puzzled):
Why aren't you wearing your uniform?

ALLEN (as if the subject isn't even worth talking about):
I couldn't wait to get out of it.[11]

He gives his mother a little hug. The others have been standing patiently by, enjoying the scene, knowing that this is Mother's big moment. Allen now looks over the rest of the group, first grasping his brother's hand warmly.

ALLEN:
Hello, Clint! You haven't changed a bit . . . (His eyes rove to Alice, who is looking at him rather embarrassed.) But *Alice*—I wouldn't have known *you*.

He takes her hand and looks at her with an expression that shows a pleasant surprise.

BROTHER:
She's grown up, hasn't she?

ALLEN:
I guess that's it . . .

ALICE (to Allen):
And you look different, too . . . I think it's the uniform I miss—it made you look *taller*—and sort of *distinguished*—

She stops as she realizes the unconscious slam. Allen gulps. It is not what he had expected by way of greeting from her. But as he sees the rest of the group, his smile returns.

ALLEN:
Say—I've got a real welcome home party here . . . Hello, fellows!

He shakes hands with several of the boys as ad lib hellos are exchanged. Then he sees his boss, who has been standing somewhat in the background. Seeing him is a great surprise.

ALLEN (extending his hand):
And *Mr. Parker!* It's awfully nice of you to be here.

BROTHER (pompously, importantly; to Allen):
You've got a lot to thank Mr. Parker for . . .

PARKER (magnanimously):
Oh, that's nothing . . .

BROTHER (to Allen; putting his arm around him):
He feels that after all you've been through we owe you something. (With pride and joy.) Mr. Parker's going to take you back into the factory.

Allen is thunderstruck at this news. It stuns him because of his different plans. Parker quickly interposes.

PARKER:
I've got the old job waiting for you . . . You've done your bit—and your boss isn't going to forget you.[12]

Everyone looks toward Allen, including Parker himself. They all expect Allen to be overjoyed at this display of magnanimity. For a minute Allen's face wears an expression of bewilderment. He knows there is no way to refuse. He starts to smile weakly, knowing it is expected of him.

DISSOLVE INTO:

15. INT. ALLEN LIVING ROOM
Allen, his mother, and brother have evidently just come in. Allen has his arm around his mother. His brother carries his kit bag. Allen throws down his hat while the brother gets rid of the bag. Then Allen gives his mother a squeeze and kisses her.

MOTHER (happily):
It's wonderful to have you back . . .

ALLEN (giving her a hug):
It's swell to be back.

BROTHER:
Let's sit down and have a talk—tell us all about the war.

ALLEN (laughing):
I won't live that long.

He sits on the arm of his mother's chair while his brother takes a comfortable armchair.

BROTHER (proudly):
What did you think of Mr. Parker being at the station?

Allen's brow furrows. He looks worried. His mother and brother are surprised as they notice this.

ALLEN (a little hesitantly):
Say, Clint—speaking of Mr. Parker—will you do me a favor?

BROTHER:
Sure . . . What is it?

ALLEN (uncomfortably):
Well—er—would you talk to him for me—and tell him I'm not going to take the job?

Allen looks from his brother to his mother. They are both shocked.

MOTHER (shocked):
Jim!

BROTHER (to Jim; puzzled):
And why should I tell him that?

ALLEN:
It's sort of hard to explain . . .

He looks toward the mother and brother but sees no understanding there.

ALLEN:

I know you don't "get" me—but the army changes a fellow . . .

16. CLOSE-UP

of Allen. He is intent on what he is trying to get over to his mother and brother.

ALLEN:

It makes you think different . . . (Rising.) I don't want to spend the rest of my life being cooped up in a shipping room—with the same routine day after day . . . I've got *ambition* . . . I want to *do* something . . . not just answer a *factory whistle* every morning instead of a *bugle call* . . .

17. WIDER ANGLE

Allen looks down at his mother. She is concerned over him. The brother wonders what has come over the kid.

MOTHER (softly):

Jim—how can you talk like that?

BROTHER (before Jim can answer):

He's tired, Mother—excited. (Putting his arm around Jim.) You don't know what you're saying—but tomorrow morning—after a good night's sleep—you'll be all ready to take up from where you left off at the factory . . . (Striking an attitude.) A soldier of peace instead of a soldier of war!

Allen shakes his head dubiously.

ALLEN:

I don't want to be a soldier of *anything*. (Earnestly.) I want to get out and do what I want to do . . . away from routine . . . routine . . . routine! I had enough of that in the army—[13] and the factory is the army right over again!

He puts his arm around his mother again, looking at her as if his eyes might make her understand, but she looks at him sorely puzzled.

BROTHER (lightly; to Allen):
I'm afraid that the glamour and glory of parades and cheering has gone a little to your head. (More seriously, with gestures becoming a sermon.) But now it's time to settle down to the real battle of life—to join the ranks of those unsung heroes who do their bit day after day in the stores—offices—factories—

ALLEN (quietly):
I want to work—but I happen to have other plans.

MOTHER (hopefully):
You mean you have another job?

ALLEN (while his mother and brother listen with no understanding of what is going on in the boy's mind):
Not exactly . . . but I've been doing engineering work, and that's what I want to do. (Enthused.) A . . . man's job . . . where you really accomplish something— (Appealing to both of them.) Construction work—where I can be out in the open—building—creating—doing things.

18. CLOSE-UP
of the brother. A grim face.

BROTHER:
That sounds very nice—but after all, a job in the hand is worth two in the bush . . .

19. WIDER ANGLE
taking in the three. Allen looks at his mother for understanding.

MOTHER (to Allen):

Your brother's right. You ought to at least *try* the factory again . . .

CLINT (to Allen):

And when you get back into the swing of the old work, you'll like it more than you think.

He smiles at Allen as if that is that. Allen does not return the smile. He is serious.

20. CLOSE-UP

of the mother. She looks longingly at the boy.

MOTHER:

And besides, some other job might take you away from me again, Jim—and I couldn't bear that . . .

21. WIDER ANGLE

taking in the three. Allen can't find words to answer his mother. She has hit his heart.

22. CLOSE-UP

of Allen and his mother. He looks toward her for the real answer.

ALLEN:

And that's how *you* really feel about it, Mom?[14]

MOTHER (looking at him tenderly):

I don't like to tell you what to do, Jim . . . but when you were in the war, every time I passed the factory—I was hoping for the day when my boy would be working there again!

She looks at Allen with such great love he cannot answer.[15]

DISSOLVE INTO:

23. CLOSE SHOT

of a factory whistle on top of a building. The whistle is blowing. Under the whistle is a large sign reading:

PARKER MANUFACTURING COMPANY
The Home of Kumfort Shoes

DISSOLVE INTO:

24. INT. SHIPPING ROOM

A small room that looks out on one side to the delivery entrance, which can be seen through the window. On the opposite side of the room is another window. Parker and Allen are standing near a desk. Allen is looking around the room which is to be his business home.

PARKER:

You see—we've moved things around quite a bit . . . This is much nicer than the old shipping room—isn't it?

ALLEN:

Yes, sir.

PARKER (pointing to the window that is near the desk):

You'll sit at this window here and check the shipments . . . The job's just about the same . . . Before you know it, you'll be doing it again with your eyes shut.

Allen nods. He is about to answer when there is a noise of a terrific explosion. Allen jumps. Parker smiles amusedly as both look toward the other window, from which direction the sound of the explosion came.

PARKER:

They're excavating— (Laughing.) I shouldn't think that would scare *you* . . .

ALLEN (now relieved and laughing too):

I was looking for the nearest dugout.

PARKER:

You'll hear lots of those explosions. (Crossing to the

window.) It's an awful nuisance. (Nodding to Allen to follow him.) They're building a new bridge over the creek. (Points.)

Allen and Parker look out of the window together, silent for a moment.

25. CLOSE-UP
Allen, shooting at his face through the window. He is looking toward the bridge that is being constructed. His eyes have an interest that has been missing until now.

26. REVERSE ANGLE
taking in Parker and Allen. Parker turns away from the window.

PARKER (goodnaturedly):
Well—looking at a construction gang doesn't make *shoes!* (He starts to leave as Allen reluctantly turns from the window.) Better get busy, Allen—file those bills of lading.

He nods toward some papers that are on the desk.

ALLEN:
Yes, sir.

Parker leaves.

27. CLOSE SHOT
Allen stands for a moment, thinking of his new surroundings. He looks at the desk. He looks toward the window that faces out onto the bridge. He hesitates, goes to the window, and looks interestedly at what is going on outside. He sighs and turns around with a look of resignation. He crosses to the desk and mechanically picks up the papers to look at them.

FADE OUT

FADE IN

28. INT. ALLEN DINING ROOM

The typical dining room of a middle-class, small-town family. Supper is just over. Places were set for three, but only the mother and brother are there. Evidently Allen has not been at supper, for his place is clean and untouched.[16] The mother watches the elder son in silence as he finishes his coffee, and then he pushes the dishes back from him—a gesture that his supper is finished. The mother starts to sweep away the crumbs and pile the dishes. This business occupies her during much of the ensuing dialogue. The silence has been ominous. Both have been thinking about Allen, and they are both worried about him.

MOTHER (worried):

It might do good if you have another talk with Jim.

BROTHER (with a sense of responsibility):

I certainly intend to. (Puzzled and nettled.) Parker's given him a job that anyone in town would grab—and what does he do? (Exasperatedly.) Day after day he checks in late from lunch—loitering around that new bridge—for no reason at all! (He shakes his head, utterly out of sympathy.)

29. CLOSE-UP

of the mother, trying to understand her boy, but she is distressed.

MOTHER:

He'll come out of it—but it worries me too . . . (Sighing.)

30. WIDER ANGLE

The brother starts to draw designs on the tablecloth with a fork; he is abstracted in thought. The mother goes silently about her work. A door slams. They look at each other.

MOTHER (calling off; making her tone lighter than her troubled mood):

That you, Jim?

ALLEN'S VOICE (off):

It's me, Mom.

MOTHER (quietly to brother):

Maybe you can speak to him now.

The brother nods. Jim comes in and perfunctorily kisses his mother as he greets his brother. He seems in low spirits—very depressed.

ALLEN:

Hello, Clint.

BROTHER:

You're quite a stranger here.

Allen shrugs.

MOTHER (to Allen):

Had supper?

ALLEN:

Wasn't hungry.

MOTHER (worried):

But you ought to have a bite of *something*.

ALLEN (dully):

I couldn't—don't feel like it . . .

BROTHER (trying not to show his annoyance):

Anyway—sit down—I want to talk to you. (Allen pulls out a chair and sits.)

ALLEN:

I want to talk to you, too.

BROTHER:

Jim. Mr. Parker's very disappointed in you . . .

31. CLOSE-UP
of Allen.[17] He listens to his brother in a sort of tolerant mood mixed with unrest.

BROTHER'S VOICE:

You haven't shown him anything. (Severely.) You know your duty's to your job . . .

Allen winces.

ALLEN:

I know it . . . but I can't help it . . . I don't know what's the matter with me.[18] (Rising nervously.)

32. WIDER ANGLE
as his mother goes over and puts her arm around him. The brother looks at him impatiently.

MOTHER (tenderly):

Maybe you're not well, dear. Why don't you go and see Dr. Whitney?

Allen shakes his head sadly.

ALLEN:

I don't need him, Mother . . . It's all up here . . . (Tapping his head, he looks tenderly at his mother, who is shocked.) I told you about it when I first came home. (With vehemence.) This isn't the kind of work I want to do . . . It's too monotonous! The whole factory's monotonous! Sometimes I feel I'd like to jump right out of my skin. (Plaintively.) I've simply got to get out of it—and get some kind of an engineering job—like I wanted to do in the first place.

He looks at his mother, hoping she will understand. She looks at him with a world of devotion; she shakes her head, sorry for him. The brother sighs impatiently. He has feared that this subject would be brought up again. He crosses to Allen.

BROTHER (to Allen):
You don't seem to realize—

ALLEN (interrupting):
That's it—realize! No one seems to realize that I am different now than when I went away. I have changed! I have seen things! I have been through hell! Here folks are concerned about my uniform—how I dance—I am out of step with everybody—all the while I was hoping to come back and start a new life—to be free—and again I find myself under orders—a drab routine—cramped, mechanical, even worse than the army and YOU— (pointing to his brother) all of you trying your darndest to map out my future—to harness me and lead me around to do what YOU think is best for ME! It doesn't occur to you that I have grown in mind and body—that I have learned that life is more important than a medal on my chest or a stupid, insignificant job![19] This town is stifling me—I've got to get out of it! I want to work, do things! Try to become something more than just a clock puncher in a small-town shoe factory!

BROTHER (interrupting):
Appreciation! That's a fine way for you—

MOTHER (interrupting):
Clint!

The brother shrugs. The mother puts her arm around Allen.

MOTHER (trying to understand the boy):
What would you do, son . . . ? Where would you go?

ALLEN (groping):
Somewhere—*anywhere* . . . where I could do the sort of work I want—building—

He becomes enthused at the idea; he is letting out his pent-up self.

33. CLOSE-UP
of the mother. She is about to make a supreme sacrifice, but she will not stand in the way of her son's happiness.

MOTHER (bravely and quietly):
If your heart's really in that, I think you certainly should follow it—

34. WIDER ANGLE
taking in the three. The brother is surprised. But Allen leaps to his feet joyously and hugs his mother.

ALLEN (to Mother):
I knew you'd understand!

She smiles ever so faintly. The brother isn't sold.

BROTHER (to Allen):
But there's hardly any construction work *here* . . . Before we know it, you'll be leaving us again.

MOTHER (before Allen can answer):
That doesn't matter . . . He's got to be happy . . . He's got to find himself.

She looks at Allen through a tear. He is all steamed up and rarin' to go.

ALLEN (to Mother, who tries her best to share his enthusiasm):
You're a peach, Mom . . . ! Listen—I know there's a lot of construction going on up in New England—and if I—

By this time we

DISSOLVE TO:

35. CLOSE-UP
of a map, showing New Jersey. We PAN OVER to the vicinity of Boston, Massachusetts. DOUBLE-EXPOSED in

this shot is a fast-moving passenger train. We hear the clickety-click of the wheels as the train speeds over the tracks.

DISSOLVE TO:

36–38. OMITTED

39. CLOSE-UP
of a large sign. The sign reads as follows: This New Million Dollar Pier under Construction by the Back Bay Engineering Co.

40. EXT. BEACH FULL SHOT
The above sign is in evidence. A pier is under construction. Several steam shovels at work near the ocean's edge.

41. CLOSE SHOT
Piloting one of these shovels is Allen, hard at his job.[20]

42. WIDER ANGLE
as the boss comes up and shouts toward Allen.

BOSS (calling):
Say, Allen!

ALLEN (shouting back):
Calling me?

BOSS (calling):
Knock off a minute. I want to see you.

Allen stops working his shovel and climbs out of it. He walks over to the boss.

BOSS:
It's bad news . . . We're cutting down—and the new men will have to go . . .

Allen's face falls but he tries to appear nonchalant.

ALLEN:

So I can kiss the job good-bye, huh?

BOSS:

I'm afraid so . . .

Allen shrugs his shoulders with forced indifference.[21]

DISSOLVE INTO:

43. CLOSE-UP OF MAP

focused on the Massachusetts area. We PAN ALONG the seacoast down to New Orleans. DOUBLE-EXPOSED in this shot is a coastwise passenger ship. We hear the deep voice of its horn as the boat plows through the water.

DISSOLVE INTO:

44. EXT. LEVEE FULL SHOT

A number of workmen are repairing a bit of the levee. A number of Negroes are mixed with the whites. (Note: If desired, the Negroes may be heard singing as they work.) Allen comes into the scene, looks around, and walks up to a man who is evidently the section boss.[22]

45. CLOSER SHOT

The section boss is biting off a wad of chewing tobacco as Allen addresses him.

ALLEN:

You the boss here?

SECTION BOSS (still trying to bite off a chaw of tobacco):

Yep.

ALLEN:

Can you use a good man?

SECTION BOSS:

Last week I could of used you—but now I'm full up.

He starts to walk away, spitting some tobacco juice and watching how far away it lands. Allen looks after him, disappointed.

DISSOLVE INTO:

46. CLOSE-UP OF MAP
focusing on New Orleans and PANNING ALONG and up to the Middle West, stopping around Wisconsin or thereabouts. DOUBLE-EXPOSED in this shot is a freight train which lumbers and rattles along.

DISSOLVE INTO:

47. MOVING SHOT
of a truck full of lumber. Allen is driving the truck. His clothes are worn. He needs a shave. Next to him sits another worker.

WORKER:
You're new here—ain't you, Buddy?

ALLEN:
I'm just filling in for a couple of days—but, believe me, I'm glad to be working . . . It's my first job in four months.

DISSOLVE INTO:

48. CLOSE-UP OF MAP
focusing on the Wisconsin and PANNING OVER to St. Louis, Missouri. DOUBLE-EXPOSED in this shot is a freight train, which lumbers and rattles along.[23]

DISSOLVE INTO:

49. CLOSE-UP
of the three balls of a pawnshop.

DISSOLVE INTO:

50. INT. PAWNSHOP
James Allen stands, thin and stooped and ragged, before the pawnbroker, holding out his medal.

ALLEN:
How much can you give me on this Belgian Croix de Guerre?

The pawnbroker silently shakes his head. He turns and opens a drawer.

51. CLOSE-UP
of the drawer. It is filled with medals of the war and other things that have been hocked by ex-soldiers.

PAWNBROKER'S VOICE:
Look—I have everything now—from German pants buttons to DSC's!

52. CLOSE SHOT
Allen and the pawnbroker. The pawnbroker closes the drawer. Allen shrugs his shoulders and wearily starts out.

DISSOLVE INTO:

53. CLOSE-UP OF MAP
focusing on St. Louis and starting to PAN south. DOUBLE-EXPOSED in this shot we see Allen walking the tracks.

DISSOLVE INTO:

54. CLOSE-UP OF A SIGN
reading

BED 15¢ MEAL 15¢ BATH 5¢

CAMERA PULLS BACK showing the anteroom of a flophouse. The room is filled with tramps, both white and colored. A clerk, standing behind a counter, is attending to those who can pay for what they want and sending them on into the interior of the building. The rest are sitting around, eyeing the others, some envious, some indifferent.

CAMERA PICKS UP Allen, seated on a bench against the wall. On one side of him is a large Negro; on the other side is Pete—hard-boiled, desperate, and a chronic bum.[24]

CAMERA DOLLIES UP to a CLOSE-UP of Allen and Pete. Both men are unshaven and filthy. Pete is playing solitaire with a dirty, greasy deck of cards. Allen sits near him and is unconsciously kibitzing. Pete cannot make any more moves with the cards and gathers them in disgustedly. He looks toward Allen for silent sympathy. Then he begins to idly shuffle the cards, and as he does so, he gives Allen a look from head to feet.

PETE:

Say, pal, how about some poker—to see who bums the handout?

ALLEN:

I'm afraid not . . . (Pete looks disappointed.) I'm new in the town—and not onto the ropes.

Pete nods understandingly. Absently he continues to shuffle the cards.

PETE:

Been on the road?

ALLEN:

Yeah . . . (With a cynical grin.) I took to walking the ties when my Hispano-Suize broke down.[25]

Pete joins Allen in a grin.

PETE:

Broke, huh?

ALLEN:

Not exactly—I have a lot of money tied up in stocks—but I don't like to sell them on a falling market.

Pete likes this guy.

PETE:

You're a cheerful sort of scout . . . What's your moniker?

ALLEN:

James Allen.

PETE:

James Allen—that'll do, I guess . . . Mine's Pete.

He holds out his hand. Allen grasps it.

ALLEN:

Glad to know you, Pete.

PETE (throwing the cards on the table):

Well—I'm hungry . . . ! What would you say to a hamburger?

ALLEN (amused):

What would I say to a hamburger? (Pete nods. Allen pretends to think deeply.) Well—I'd shake Mr. Hamburger by the hand—and I'd say, "You're an old friend—but I haven't seen you in a long, long time."

PETE:

I think I can mooch a couple in the lunch wagon down the street. The guy who runs it is a pretty soft egg . . . What do you say?

ALLEN (his face lighting):

I hope you're not fooling.

He starts to get up to join Pete.

DISSOLVE INTO:

55. INT. OF A LUNCH WAGON

A lone customer is finishing his coffee. Mike, the proprietor, is standing behind the counter. Pete and Allen stand in front of the counter.

PETE (to Mike):

How about giving me and my friend a handout?

Mike is not pleased, but he is softhearted.

MIKE:

I was hoping you'd left town.

PETE (coaxingly):

Say—I been laying off of you for a couple of days . . . Come on—be a sport.

Mike shakes his head and sighs.

MIKE:
All right—sit over there.

He nods to a corner of the lunch wagon. Pete gives Allen a broad wink, and Allen smiles thankfully at his new friend. They go to the corner of the lunch wagon and sit down.

56. CLOSE-UP OF MIKE
as he slaps out two hamburgers and puts them on the fire.

57. CLOSE-UP OF ALLEN
as he sees the hamburgers sizzling. He licks his lips in anticipation of the coming feast.

58. WIDER ANGLE
taking in all. The customer has finished his coffee. He gets up.

CUSTOMER (to Mike):
What do I owe you?

MIKE:
Fifteen cents.

The customer puts the money on the counter and leaves. Mike takes the money and steps over to the cash register, which is close to the boys. He rings it up. A few dollar bills are visible.

59. CLOSE-UP OF PETE
as he casually glances toward the cash register. It gives him a thought. A cunning expression creeps over his face.

60. WIDER ANGLE
taking in all. Mike is just about to close the cash register when Pete's voice arrests him.

PETE:

Business is pretty good, huh?

MIKE (puzzled):

Yeah. Pretty good.

PETE (his voice suddenly becoming hard):

How good?

Pete whips a gun out of his pocket and points it at Mike.

MIKE (staring at the gun):

Hey—what is this?

PETE:

Put your hands on the counter. (Mike complies.) Lean over here—just like you and me are talking.

Mike does what he is told. He leans across the counter by Pete; the gun is almost against his heart. Allen sits staring, dazed. Pete turns to him.

PETE (to Allen):

Get the dough out of the cash register.

ALLEN:

Listen—

PETE:

Go on. Do as I say . . .

He turns the gun a little so that it covers Allen. Allen slowly gets off the stool and moves around to the cash register. He hesitates.

PETE (gesturing with the gun):

Come on!

He looks at the gun again. Then he takes the money out of the till, his hand shaking a little.

PETE (to Allen):

How much is there?

The sweat has come out on Mike's face. He moves to wipe it off. Pete knocks his hand down.

ALLEN (counting):
Five dollars—and eighty cents.

PETE (angrily to Mike):
There ought to be more than that! Where is it?

MIKE (nervously):
No—no—that's all—

Pete gives him a fierce look, then turns to Allen.

PETE:
Put the dough in your pocket and come on.

Pete starts backing toward the door, keeping the gun on both Mike and Allen. By the door he reaches up with one hand and yanks the telephone cord from its socket.

PETE (to Mike):
And don't start yelling for the cops—

He is interrupted by a voice from outside.

VOICE:
You won't have to yell, Mike.

Pete whirls around in the doorway and shoots. There is another shot, and Pete crumples. Two cops walk in, guns in their hands. Allen stands helpless. The two cops step forward excitedly to see whether or not Pete is killed. As they bend over, Allen, in a panic, makes a dash for the doorway.[26]

MIKE (excitedly, from behind the counter):
Get that guy—he's got the money!

The cops whirl around. One of them makes a grab at Allen as Allen tries to slip out of the door. With a terrific shove he manages to push the cop away from him and runs out. The cops immediately start after him.

61. FULL SHOT
of street as Allen runs desperately with the cops not far behind him. Just as he gets to a corner,

62. CLOSE SHOT OF A CORNER
showing the street that runs right angles to the one in the above scene. A moment with no figures, then Allen rounds the corner and rushes past the camera. Another moment with no figures, then the cops round the corner in pursuit.

63. FULL SHOT OF THIS SECOND STREET
Allen being pursued by the cops. They have gained slightly on him.

64. MED. SHOT
as Allen is about to turn in an alley. There is a brick wall behind him.

65. CLOSE SHOT OF ONE OF THE COPS
stopping and leveling a revolver. He pulls the trigger.

66. CLOSE SHOT OF ALLEN
as a bullet hits the brick wall right over his head. He ducks in fright as a second bullet hits the wall. If he hadn't ducked it would have plugged him. As he tries to regain his feet to run away—

67. MED. SHOT
As Allen gets to his feet the cops are on him. They grab him roughly.

FADE OUT

FADE IN

68. INT. COURTROOM MED. CLOSE-UP OF JUDGE
seated upon the bench, with the back of Allen's head in the foreground.

JUDGE (as though summing up the case):
I see no reason for leniency—since the money was found on your person. Furthermore, upon detection, you attempted to escape—which would of necessity increase the seriousness of your offense. (He

commences rapping on the desk with his gavel.) I therefore, in accordance with the laws of this state, sentence you to ten years of hard labor—[27]

Throughout this speech and during the pounding of the gavel, we

69. CLOSE-UP OF THE GAVEL
rapping for order. From the pounding gavel,

DISSOLVE TO:

70. CLOSE-UP A SMALL SLEDGE HAMMER (PRISON BLACKSMITH SHOP)
pounding in the rivet that fastens the shackles and chains to one of the legs of James Allen. CAMERA PULLS BACK to show Allen, in striped prison suit, staring down at the chains. Allen seems bewildered, dazed.[28] The blacksmith finishes the job and looks at the strong shackles proudly, taking a sadistic delight in his work. Mr. Blacksmith sinisterly counts off the links.

BLACKSMITH (counting):

One—two—three—four—five—six—seven—eight—nine—ten—eleven—twelve—thirteen . . . A nice lucky number!

Allen stares down at his shackles. He notices the three-foot chain which is fastened to the chain between his legs, the loose end of which is lying on the floor. He picks it up gingerly and examines the iron ring on the end.

ALLEN (glancing at the blacksmith and indicating the loose chain):

What's this for?

BLACKSMITH:

To pick your teeth with.[29] (He grabs a pair of prison shoes from the bench and throws them down at Allen's feet.) Here—take off your shoes.

Allen drops the chain. It clanks on the floor as he bends over and starts removing his shoes.

DISSOLVE TO:

71. CLOSE-UP ALLEN'S HANDS
lacing up the heavy prison shoes on his feet. The shoes are much too large. The old army shoes lie sprawled beside him. One of the shoes is turned upside down, showing the sole worn through.

VOICE (outside shot; hard and gutteral):
Get a move on.

Allen has finished tying the laces of his shoes. CAMERA PULLS BACK showing a guard standing in the doorway. Allen rises and starts to walk but at the first step he almost trips himself, inasmuch as only a little over a half-step can be taken on account of the chain.

GUARD (gruffly):
Pick it up.

Allen pauses and stares at the guard. He is bewildered, dazed, not realizing yet where he is. It is a bad dream.

GUARD:
Pick up that chain!

Allen glances at his feet and notices the upright chain with the loose end lying on the floor. He stoops down and picks it up.

GUARD:
Follow me.

He goes out the door. It is almost dusk. Through the doorway, the faint glow that is still in the sky can be seen. Allen, with his back to the CAMERA, shuffles out through the door slowly and off as the scene

FADES OUT

FADE IN

72. SLEEPING QUARTERS DARK

A chain clanks in the darkness. Then a lamp appears in the foreground, and we see silhouetted black against it two guards. One of them passes on down the room, and in the light from his lamp we see dimly the figures of convicts sprawled on cots. The guard with the lamp unlocks the building chain, which runs the length of the room and to which the sleeping men are fastened by their upright chains.

GUARD (yelling):

Get up—and I mean *you!* [30]

The convicts sit up in bed, each one grabbing the ring of his upright chain. The guard in the foreground starts pulling on the building chain, and it runs noisily through the rings held by the men.

73. JAMES ALLEN

still lying asleep on his cot. The noise of the chains arouses him, and he sits up, blinking bewilderedly in the semidarkness. He is suddenly jerked out of his cot and crashes against the next cot. He lies there a little stunned. The guard with the lamp comes up and loosens the building chain which has caught in the ring of Allen's upright chain.

GUARD:

That'll learn you to sit up and hold onto *this!*

The guard throws the upright ring into Allen's face.

74. FULL SHOT

The other guard pulls the building chain through the rest of the rings. The convicts, fully dressed, drag bodies, aching with weariness, off their cots and move heavily in a mass toward the next room.[31]

75. MESS ROOM

The convicts coming in. They move sluggishly. The room is dimly lit by lamps that throw a yellow jaundiced light. There is a long table with benches running down each side. The first men in grab seats on the ends of the benches. The others must first sit with their backs to the table, then swing both chained legs around together over the bench. They sit heavily on the crude benches.

James Allen pauses a moment, sees what the others do, then sits on a bench and swings his legs over. He looks around him.

The faces of the convicts, stained by the sickly light, are grim and grotesque. A sullen silence hangs heavily, broken only by an occasional animallike snarl as one man jostles against another in getting into place, or as a man is faced again with the same horrible food.

There is a tin plate in front of each man. On it are a piece of fried dough, three small pork sides, and some sorghum, beside it a cup of black coffee. Allen is still bewildered and dazed as he glances around the table and looks down at the food in front of him.

76. CLOSE-UP OF ALLEN

He mechanically puts his fork into the food and takes a mouthful.[32] He starts to chew and the taste of the food sickens him. He lays down his fork and pushes the plate away from him. He is on the verge of nausea.

77. WIDER ANGLE

as the convicts around him look at him. One of them laughs uproariously. Another nudges his neighbor and nods toward Allen. Allen stares blankly at the unappetizing food in front of him.

Sitting next to Allen is Bomber Wells, a large, violent man with a grim sense of humor. He is up for life and has already spent twelve years on the chain gang. He is completely hardened to it now. A pork side in his mouth, chewing with his mouth open, he turns and looks at Allen.

BOMBER:

Grease, fried dough, pig fat, and sorghum. You better like it—because you're going to get the same thing every morning—every year.

BARNEY:

You can't get better food on any chain gang in the state—

BOMBER:

Yeah . . . And you can go all over the world—and never find worse . . .

ALLEN:

They don't think anybody can eat a mess like this, do they?

Allen starts trying to eat it again. He takes a bit; his face lines with distaste. He shoves the plate away with finality.

Across the table is Barney Sykes, shifty eyed, black haired—a sheik in convict's clothing. He always tries to be one of the tough boys. He takes up the note of defiance. He takes a drink of his coffee. He spits it out.

BOMBER:

Why do you keep on trying that slime if you're going to spit it out every morning?

BARNEY:

I'm practicing. The last day of my year here I'm going to spit it right in the warden's kisser.

BOMBER:

He'll be blinded for life . . .

Allen listens, still as if he were having a nightmare and expected to wake up. Across the table from Allen is Red, a young man with face not yet hardened. He is chewing.

He stops suddenly, his face pale and lined with nausea. He gulps. Then his head falls onto his arms on the table. His body shudders.[33]

DISSOLVE TO:

78. THE PRISON YARD

weirdly lighted with a few glare torches, enclosed by two separate fences of barbed wire. The warden stands in the doorway of the building, shouting.

WARDEN:

Come by me. Come by me.[34]

The men file out of the building. They move faster now, but still heavily, their chains clanking.

79. SECOND BUILDING

Negroes filing out, chains clanking, their black skins shining in the torchlight.

80. THE PRISON YARD

The men assemble in groups of twenty, lined up two by two. The Negroes form their separate groups.

James Allen follows Bomber Wells. The men line up side by side, each holding his upright chain toward the man next to him. Allen and Bomber line up together. The guards have started running "squad chain" down the center of each group, passing the squad chain through each iron ring so that twenty men are chained together and each man can move only about five feet from his nearest neighbor. There is no talk, no noise except the clanking of chains.

81. A SERIES OF CLOSE-UPS

James Allen, bewildered, wondering. Nordine, his vicious eyes alert, darting. Red, his face pale and sick. A resigned, beaten, white face. A hard, bitter face. A sullen white face. Expressionless black faces. Each seen for a moment in the flickering flare of the torches.

82. CLOSE-UP (TO INTERCUT WITH ABOVE)
The squad chain being run through the iron rings, chaining the men together.

83. ANOTHER PART OF THE YARD
A team of four mules, lined up two by two, being fastened together, like the convicts.

84. FULL SHOT OF YARD
The groups, chained together now, are climbing onto the trucks. At the gate, each truck with a driver and two guards with guns on their laps on the front seat stops while the men are counted. Then the truck moves out.

DISSOLVE TO:

85. ROCK QUARRY AT DAWN
In the first dim light of dawn we see dark figures huddled among the rocks, waiting for light enough to work.

86. GROUP ALLEN, BOMBER, NORDINE
They sprawl together by a large rock. Nordine is a small, vicious-looking man. He leans over and touches Allen on the arm.[35] Allen starts. He is still not part of his surroundings.

NORDINE:
Are you up here for murder, kid?

ALLEN:
No . . .

NORDINE (worried):
I heard that a guy that killed four people was being sent up here.

BOMBER:
Nordine's always worrying about losing his spot as high man here—he only killed three . . .

NORDINE:
More than anyone else in this chain gang . . .[36]

BOMBER:

His wife, sister-in-law, and mother-in-law . . . Killed 'em in one night—with an ax—so he wouldn't disturb the neighbors . . .

NORDINE (to Allen; still suspicious):

What *are* you up taking the rap for?

ALLEN:

I didn't do anything.[37]

The men wink at each other and laugh.

BOMBER (with rough good nature; to Allen):

Come on—tell us—you're among friends.

Allen looks at his "friends" with an attempted smile that misses.

87. FULL SHOT OF THE QUARRY

A GUARD (shouting):

Get to work! And I mean you![38]

The dark, huddled figures rise and start moving. Their chains clank on the rocks. Their bent figures are silhouetted against the glowing east as they commence working. Sledges start to rise and fall—the noise of drills, men breaking up large rocks, the clanking of chains, and the ring of the hammering sledges. The first rays of the sun flash from a swinging sledge at the top of its arc.

DISSOLVE TO:

88. QUARRY MIDDAY

The hot sun glaring down, sledges still swinging, bodies sweating and steaming, guards watching, wandering about, finding fault with everybody's work. Ad lib. "No one works hard enough." The only answer allowed from the convicts is "Yes, sir." A convict stops working and shouts to the nearest guard.

CONVICT:

Getting out here.

The guard points to a clump of bushes at the side of the quarry.

GUARD:

All right—get out there.

The convict goes to the clump of bushes.

89. ALLEN AND BOMBER

swinging their sledges in synchronization, driving in the same drill. Without stopping work, Allen nods at the convict going into the bushes.

ALLEN:

What's the idea?

BOMBER:

He gets two minutes— (He spits through his teeth.) To brush his teeth.

Allen nods understandingly.

90. SEBASTIAN YALE

A huge Negro, swinging his sledge with beautiful rhythm and perfect accuracy. He is not far from Allen and Bomber.

91. ALLEN AND BOMBER

Bomber nods toward the big Negro.

BOMBER:

Look at that big buck handle a sledge. He never misses . . . You can lay down a nickel and he'll knock the buffalo's right eye out.

Allen looks dully toward the Negro and nods to Bomber mechanically.

BOMBER:

They like his work so much they're going to keep him here the rest of his life.

He laughs at his own joke as Allen continues to stare at the Negro.

92. CLOSE-UP ALLEN

as he starts to wipe the sweat off his face. A fist enters, crashing against Allen's jaw, knocking him out of the shot.

93. CLOSE SHOT

Allen lies sprawled on the ground. A guard towers over him. Bomber keeps on swinging his sledge. Allen's hand tightens on his sledge.[39] Before he can swing it Bomber's foot steps on it, the Bomber still swinging his sledge.

GUARD:

Quit stalling—come on, get up . . .

ALLEN (rising):

I just wanted to get the sweat off my face . . .

GUARD:

Well, you got it knocked off.

The guard moves away.

94. CLOSE-UP OF ALLEN

He looks aggressively after the guard. He "sees red." He starts toward him when Bomber's detaining hand comes into the scene.

95. CLOSE SHOT

Bomber shakes his head at Allen.

BOMBER:

That won't do no good . . . You got to *ask permission* to wipe the sweat off— (Calling out.) Wiping it off . . .

GUARD'S VOICE:

All right, Bomber—wipe it off.

Bomber stops and wipes off the sweat.

BOMBER:

Like that . . . and in the first place, you got to get their permission to sweat . . .

He resumes swinging his sledge.

96. RED

He is sagging. He tries to swing his sledge, but his arms won't work anymore. A guard comes up. Red looks at him pitifully.

RED (gasping):

I got to quit . . . my stomach . . .

GUARD:

Get to work or I'll kick that bellyache up around your ears.

Red trembles, then starts swinging his sledge weakly. CAMERA PULLS BACK to show the whole quarry.[40] Sledges swinging under the blazing sun, black men and white men, the guards prodding them to work harder, an occasional "Yes, sir," a man calling "Wiping it off," and the answering "Wipe it off," the clank of sledges and chains. A figure crumples to the ground.

GUARD (yelling):

Keep on working . . .

97. CLOSE-UP RED

Red lies unconscious on the ground. A bucket of warm water is thrown in his face. He does not stir. A foot comes in and kicks him.[41]

FADE OUT

FADE IN

98. PRISON YARD[42] DUSK

Several of the trucks have already arrived as others drive in. The men are climbing off the trucks and the squad chains are being removed. Allen and Bomber Wells are among the men.

99. CLOSE SHOT SQUAD

including Allen and Bomber. The men are caked with dust and sweat. They are dead tired, their shoulders sagging, their heads drooping. A guard is removing the squad chain. They then go into the building.

100. ANOTHER PART OF THE YARD

The group of mules being unfastened, like the convicts, after their day's work.

101. CLOSE-UP OF FEET AND LEGS OF FIRST CONVICT

in front of one of the guards.[43] He is standing with his feet apart and the chain drawn tight between them. The guard, seated on a little stool, bends down to examine the links of the chain to see that they haven't been tampered with, as well as the ankle bracelets. As soon as the guard is satisfied with his inspection, he says: "All right." The convict calls out "One" as he enters the building and the next man in line takes his place in front of the guard. The guard examines his chains and says, "All right," and the second man, calling out "Two," enters the building. We hold this scene long enough to become acquainted with the routine.

CUT TO:

102. INT. PRISON BUILDING

at the door as the convicts file in from the prison yard. Here they pass another guard who examines them for signs of perspiration. He smells each convict in turn and then, satisfied that the convict has done a hard day's work, he nods him to go on.

CUT TO:

103. INT. MESS HALL

starting with a CLOSE-UP on a large bowl of water, dirty and thick. Two men have their hands in the black water. Another puts his grimy hands in it. (The men wash in a corner of the mess hall.)[44]

The CAMERA PULLS BACK and we see it is the only facility for washing. Allen and Bomber come from the doorway. Allen stops and looks around. He is surprised at these conditions, but by now is resigned to anything. He almost smiles—a bitter smile.

ALLEN (unbelievingly):
Is this the washroom?

BOMBER:
Yep.

Bomber steps up to the basin and starts to wash. He turns toward Allen.

BOMBER:
Come on—there's room.

Allen cannot bring himself to wash in that muck. He shakes his head.

ALLEN:
Nope—I forgot my bath salts.

He goes toward the dining room table.

104. A TIN PLATE OF FOOD

The food is the same as breakfast—a little worse. CAMERA PANS UP as Allen swings his feet around to face the table. He stares down at the lousy food, then up at the convicts. They are all eating voraciously.

CUT TO:

105. SLEEPING QUARTERS

Red staggers in and throws himself on a cot. He lies there shuddering.

CUT TO:

106. MESS TABLE

The silence is heavy. There is no note of defiance now—everybody is too tired and hungry. Even James Allen eats, like the rest. He eats eagerly—fat, pork, and all.

DISSOLVE TO:

107. INT. SLEEPING QUARTERS

Allen lies exhausted on his cot. Other men are sprawled on their beds. Everyone is too tired to talk as they lie there in their sweaty clothes.

108. CLOSE-UP

Allen, now that he has time to think, is utterly dejected. It is like a terrible nightmare as he looks around him.

WARDEN'S VOICE:

All right, boys—show me the men that didn't give us a good day's work.

At the sound of this harsh voice Allen shuts his eyes as if to blot out grim reality.

109. FULL SHOT

The warden, with a group of guards, is walking along the line of cots. He has a leather strap six feet long, three inches wide, a quarter of an inch thick.

110. CLOSE-UP

Allen, opening his eyes and watching what they intend to do.

111. WIDER ANGLE

The group moves down the row of beds. They come to Ackerman, gaunt and thin.

GUARD:

Ackerman here hasn't been on the job, Warden.

WARDEN:

Is that so?

The warden jerks his head toward the mess room. Ackerman rises slowly, his face a mask of horror as he moves toward the door. One of the convicts removes Ackerman's shirt. The group goes on down the line.

WARDEN:

Anybody else?

FIRST GUARD (to warden):

Red. He tried to pull a faint.

112. CLOSE-UP OF RED

on a cot, as the warden bends over him, grabs him by the shoulder, and turns him face up.

RED (miserably):

I don't care what you do to me—it doesn't matter.

WARDEN:

Oh—so that's the way you feel . . . Well—take a look at this.

He holds the leather strap in front of Red's face. Red's eyes grow wide. He shudders.

113. CLOSE SHOT

Allen and Wilson, the man in the next cot.

ALLEN (to Wilson; in a whisper before he realizes what he has said):

The skunk!

114. CLOSE-UP

the warden, looking up quickly.

115. CLOSE-UP ALLEN

on his cot. He looks up now with a slight trace of defiance as he realizes the warden has overheard him.

116. CLOSE-UP

of the warden and the guards staring at Allen, a cruel leer on the warden's face.

WARDEN:

You're next. (He turns to a guard.) Take his stinking shirt off.

The warden turns and walks out of the room.

117. CLOSE-UP OF ALLEN

showing two guards pulling his shirt off, dragging him to his feet, and walking him down the corridor toward the door. They pause outside the door, Allen with his bare back to the CAMERA. There is a moment of absolute silence; then from the mess room can be heard the terrific crash of leather on bare skin. Allen, standing rigid, winces instinctively at every crash of the leather—one . . . two . . . three . . . four . . . (at the end of the fourth blow an exclamation finally escapes the unseen figure of Ackerman in the next room) . . . five . . . six . . . seven. At this point, Ackerman loses all control and lets out an excruciating scream . . . eight . . . nine . . . ten.

118. FULL SHOT OF THE MEN ON THE COTS

CAMERA PANS DOWN the line from one to another, showing various expressions of fear, dumb horror, resentment, and occasionally an expression of smug satisfaction on the features of a convict who is relieved by the thought that someone else is being beaten instead of him.

119. DOORWAY

Allen standing there. Two guards push past him, dragging the half-conscious figure of Ackerman, limp and bleeding. Allen stares at him.

WARDEN'S VOICE:

Take your shirt, dummy.

Ackerman's shirt flies out the door. The two guards jerk Allen in through the doorway.

120. CLOSE-UP BOMBER

staring toward the door. CAMERA MOVES UP past the other convicts, all staring toward the empty doorway in morbid fascination. The crash of the leather on bare flesh is heard as the CAMERA MOVES slowly toward the open door.[45] On the fourth crash of leather, just as the CAMERA STARTS THROUGH THE DOOR, the scene

FADES OUT

FADE IN

121. A CALENDAR

The warden's leather strap crashes across the calendar. A month is swept off.

DISSOLVE TO:

122. SHOOTING INTO A PRISON WINDOW

Convicts' faces are peering out. Allen is there, also Bomber, Wilson, Doggy, and others. They look out hungrily.

123. SHOOTING OUT THROUGH THE WINDOW

Past the convicts looking out through the bars, Barney is seen in street clothes as he passes out the heavy gate.[46] He gives the guard at the gate a farewell salute that is very close to nose thumbing. From habit he still walks with the short chain gang step.

124. INT. SLEEPING QUARTERS

as most of the men slowly turn away from the window. A few still look after the departed Barney. Everyone wishes he were Barney.

WILSON:

Well, Barney's gone.

DOGGY:

The lucky rat.

ALLEN:

At least it proves something—you really can get out of here!

DOGGY:

Sure you can. (Pointing to some marks on the wall beside his bed.) And I keep track of the days. They ain't gonna cheat me out of anything.

BOMBER:

When's your time up?

DOGGY:

I got it figured out exactly. (Consulting the wall.) Four days—two weeks—seven months . . . and twelve years.

They all give hollow laughs.

ALLEN (half to himself):

Let's see . . . Four weeks from ten years . . . That's nine years and forty-eight weeks.

WILSON (with a short laugh):

You can't count those away.

Allen lowers his head slowly and gazes at his ankles. Then he looks out of the window again. Wilson is standing near the window.

WILSON (grimly; nodding toward the window):

Red's leaving today, too.

CUT TO:

125. EXT. PRISON YARD SHOOTING OUT THROUGH THE WINDOW

A coffin is being hoisted into a truck.[47] Then the truck starts out.

CUT TO:

126. INT. SLEEPING QUARTERS

The men's faces become grim and bitter. Wilson and Allen turn away from the window, restraining their emotions with silence.

BOMBER:

Well—that's two ways to get out of here . . . Work out and die out . . .

127. THE ROAD NEAR THE CAMP CLOSE SHOT
Barney. A prison truck has drawn up alongside of him, the motor still running.

GUARD (on the truck):
You might as well grab a ride into town with us . . .

BARNEY:
Yeah . . . I can't walk very good anymore without those chains on.

Barney climbs on the back of the truck. There is the coffin containing Red. He sits on it and slowly lights a cigarette.[48]

128. INT. SLEEPING QUARTERS
The men are going over to their cots, too concerned over the events of the day to do much talking. Allen stands brooding. Wilson is near him.

ALLEN:
Doesn't a man ever break loose?

WILSON:
You mean hang it on the limb . . . ? (He shakes his head sadly.) There's too many breaks against you. You've got to beat the chains—the bloodhounds—and a bunch of guards who'd just as soon bring you back dead.

He walks away from Allen. Bomber has been listening to the conversation from his cot. He nods to Allen. Allen goes over.

129. CLOSE SHOT
Bomber and Allen.

BOMBER (quietly):
It might be done—but you got to figure out some perfect scheme.

130. CLOSE-UP
Allen looking intently toward the window.

BOMBER'S VOICE:
> You got to watch—you got to wait—maybe a year—maybe two—then hang it on the limb.

Allen is thinking hard to himself.

FADE OUT

FADE IN

131. THE CALENDAR AGAIN
A number of sledges superimposed, pounding in rapid rhythm. With each stroke a month flies off, until several months have passed.

DISSOLVE TO:

132. ONE SLEDGE
crashing against the rails of an old rusty railroad track. The blows land with terrific force, jarring the rails loose.

CAMERA PULLS BACK. It is the giant Negro, Sebastian Yale, swinging the sledge. Allen is working close to him. Allen stops a moment and looks around.

CAMERA PANS AROUND and picks up the chain gang, both white and colored, working together on the railroad bed. They are tearing up the rails, ties and all. The guards at either end of the gang seem weary and are paying very little attention to the men.

133. EXT. BY TRACKS CLOSE SHOT
Three bloodhounds sit beneath a tree, chained, panting with the terrific heat. A guard sits drowsily nearby, having a hard time to keep his eyes open in the heavy humidity.

134. ALLEN AND SEBASTIAN
They are a little separated from the other convicts.

ALLEN (cautiously):
> Sebastian . . .

SEBASTIAN:
Yas, suh. (He keeps on swinging his sledge.)

ALLEN:
Do you think you can hit my shackles hard enough to bend them?

Sebastian stares at him, still swinging his sledge, every blow landing true.

SEBASTIAN (his mouth agape):
You thinkin' about—

ALLEN (interrupting):
I've been thinking about it for months. If you can bend my shackles just a little, I can slide them off my foot . . .

SEBASTIAN (undecided):
Ah don't want to get in no trouble—but ah'd certainly like to see you get away from this misery.

ALLEN:
The heat's got the guards down—

Sebastian looks toward the guards and nods.

SEBASTIAN:
All right, boss—but you keep your eye on them . . .

ALLEN:
I am— Look—I'll put my leg like this . . .[49]

Allen puts his shackles against the end of a railroad tie.

SEBASTIAN:
Hold still now . . . If I hit your leg your foot will drop off right along with the shackle . . . (He grins.)

Sebastian has grown so absorbed at the idea that he is about to stop working.

SEBASTIAN:

You got to promise not to yell no matter how it hurts—or they'll accuse me of helping you.

ALLEN:

I promise . . . (With a warning glance in the direction of the guard.) Better keep working . . . I'm leaving my foot here—see? You hit it when you can.

135. CLOSE-UP OF ALLEN'S FOOT

up against the end of the railroad tie so that the shackle is pressing against the wood. His other foot is placed a few inches forward, in order to leave room for the sledge to hit the exposed side of the shackle. Sebastian's sledge can be heard falling with resounding crashes on the ties.

136. MED. SHOT OF THE GROUP

showing all the convicts working and the two guards at either end completely unaware that anything is wrong. Sebastian, seizing the opportunity, brings his sledge down against the shackle with terrific force. Allen can be seen to start slightly from the shock.

137. ALLEN AND SEBASTIAN

Allen takes a deep breath and shuts his eyes. Sebastian swings the sledge. It crashes against the shackle. Allen's whole body is jarred. He looks at the shackle—then at the guards.

ALLEN:

Again . . .

Sebastian swings twice more.

ALLEN:

Now the other one . . .

He puts the other shackle against the end of the rail.

138. CLOSE-UP
of the shackle as the sledge crashes against it.

DISSOLVE TO:

139. INT. MESS ROOM AT OUTER DOORWAY
The guard sitting on the stool examining the shackles, the men lined up outside the door. Allen is the third in line. The other men are stooped and detached—it is just the old routine to them, meaningless. Allen is tense and rigid. The two men in front of him are passed in.

140. CLOSE-UP
The guard's hands on Allen's shackles, giving them a perfunctory examination. There is no evident change in the shackles.

141. CLOSE-UP ALLEN
His face tense, not daring to look down.

GUARD'S VOICE:
All right . . .

Allen's face relaxes. He starts on in.

DISSOLVE TO:

142. CLOSE-UP
In the dim darkness Allen's hands working the shackle slowly over the heel. It sticks. CAMERA PULLS BACK. Allen wets the heel with spit. The shackle slides off. Bomber's face appears close, seen faintly in the darkness.

BOMBER:
When are you going to do it?

ALLEN:
Monday . . .

BOMBER:
That's good. You can rest up for it on Sunday. (A pause. Then.) Got any dough?

ALLEN:
A little . . .

BOMBER:
Here's seven bucks. (He takes some bills out of his shirt and hands them to Allen.) When you get to Stanton look up Barney . . . Here's his address . . . (He hands Allen a slip of paper.) He'll take care of you . . .

ALLEN:
Thanks, Bomber.

BOMBER:
Nervous?

ALLEN:
A little.

BOMBER (sincerely):
Well—no matter what happens . . . it's better than this . . .

Allen nods.

FADE OUT

FADE IN

143. LONG SHOT SHOOTING FROM AN ELEVATION
down on a bridge in the process of being demolished by the chain gang. Only a single strand of the bridge is left between the two banks of the small stream. On either side of the road that crosses the stream at this point are bushes and shrubbery about four feet high, and in the distance heavily wooded hills and tangled swamps stretch as far as the eye can see. On one side of the stream are nine convicts, one guard, and three bloodhounds. On the other side James Allen, Bomber Wells, another convict, and one guard are working.

144. CLOSE SHOT
of Allen's side of the stream.

ALLEN (to Wells, after looking around carefully):
What do you think?

BOMBER (casually):
Looks pretty good to me.

Allen glances once more at Wells as though seeking some sort of assurance. He hesitates a moment, then takes a deep breath and calls out to the guard.

ALLEN:
Getting out here!

The guard, who is several feet away, glances over his shoulder at the bushes alongside of the road.

GUARD (pointing out a certain spot in the bushes):
All right. Get out there.

Allen turns, walks off the road and into the bushes.

145. CLOSE SHOT IN BUSHES
James Allen sits down and starts to hurriedly take off his shoes.

146. STREAM
The others go on working. The guard has turned back to watch them.

147. BUSHES
James Allen has his shoes and socks off now. He is working the shackle off. He gets the first one off. The second sticks at the heel. He tries to wet it with saliva, but his mouth is dry from the work and his present nervous tenseness. He works feverishly. Finally he gets it off. He starts putting his shoes and socks back on.

148. STREAM
The guard glances toward the bushes into which Allen disappeared. Bomber sees him looking and calls his at-

tention to something he is working on, on the last supports of the bridge.

BOMBER:
Hey, boss—what do we do about this?

The guard turns to Wells.

149. BUSHES
Allen finishes tying on his shoes. He starts crawling away through the bushes.

150. BUSHES ANOTHER SETUP
Allen crawling toward the CAMERA on his hands and knees, his face set, tense.

GUARD'S VOICE:
Come on, Allen—back to work.

For just a flash Allen hesitates. Then he jumps up.

151. BUSHES MED. SHOT
as Allen jumps up and runs toward the trees.

152. STREAM
The guard stares in surprise for a moment. Then he raises his gun.

153. BUSHES
Allen running—he has almost reached the trees. There is the sound of a gun firing, and buckshot splatters all around him. He reaches the trees in safety.

154. STREAM
Everybody has stopped work and is looking after Allen.

FIRST GUARD (calling to other guard across stream):
Get the dogs— We'll have that guy back in half an hour.

The second guard runs to unleash the dogs. The first guard calls to them, and they splash across the stream to him. He starts with them toward where Allen went into the bushes.

155. WOODS

Allen running along, crashing through the underbrush.

156. BUSHES

The guard follows.

157. NEAR THE STREAM

The second guard unleashes the dogs. They start yelping and running.[50]

158. WOODS

Allen crashing through the underbrush.

159. WOODS

The dogs coming on, yelping.

160. WOODS

Allen hears the yelping and knows that the dogs have picked up the scent. He runs on faster.

DISSOLVE INTO:

161. A SMALL CLEARING

in the woods. There is a small Negro shack in the clearing. On a crude clothesline are several gingham dresses, several men's shirts, and a pair of overalls.

James Allen peers cautiously out of the brush at the edge of the clearing. There is no one in sight. He rushes to the clothesline and tears off a shirt and the overalls.

A dog yelps from off-scene very close. Allen starts, frightened. The dog, a mangy cur, runs around the corner of the cabin.

James Allen dashes back into the woods with the clothes.

162. WOODS
The bloodhounds coming on.

163. THICKET
James Allen stops and starts tearing off his striped convict clothes. The yelping of the dogs keeps getting closer.

164. WOODS
The hounds coming on, yelping. The second guard, with the hounds, has caught up to the other guard.

165. THICKET
James Allen pulls the overalls on. The howling of the hounds is very close now. He starts on furiously.

DISSOLVE TO:

166. SWAMPLAND
James Allen fighting his way through the muck. The sun shines down brutally. He wipes the sweat from his face without stopping. The howling of the dogs is close now.

167. SWAMPLAND
The dogs coming on, yelping, followed by the guards.

168. SWAMPLAND
James Allen fights his way on, frantically.

169. SWAMPLAND
The guards coming on, slowly, confident of the dogs yelping a ways in front of them. They are calm in contrast to Allen's frenzy. They plod on relentlessly, guns under their arms.

170. SWAMPLAND
James Allen fighting his way through the muck, frenziedly. He keeps sinking into the muck. The yelping of the dogs is very close now. He falls, gets up, and rushes on.

DISSOLVE TO:

171. SWAMPLAND NEAR RIVER
The dogs are just a few yards behind James Allen now, howling louder. He fights on toward the river.

172. SWAMPLAND
The guards coming on. They grin at the howling of the dogs. They know they are on Allen's heels.

173. RIVERBANK
There is some bamboo growing along the edge of the river. A desperate idea comes to Allen. He breaks off a large bamboo shoot. He looks at it quickly, then he blows through it to test it; it will do. He runs into the water and submerges himself.

174. CLOSE-UP
shooting on the water as Allen disappears beneath it. The bamboo shoot slowly emerges, too, until only about an inch of it appears above the water. It remains this way. We hear the yelping of the dogs.

175. UNDERWATER SHOT
Allen is under the water. With one hand he clings onto a stump for support. In the other hand he holds the bamboo shoot. One end of the shoot is in his mouth. The other end protrudes above the water. He breathes through it.

176. FULL SHOT
as the guards and the dogs reach the riverbank. The dogs yelp and jump around. The guards beat around the brush. They can find no trace of Allen and they are puzzled.

177. UNDERWATER SHOT
Allen, under the water, is apparently safe as he gets his air through the bamboo shoot.

178. CLOSE SHOT

of the guards sorely puzzled. The dogs continue their noise. One of the guards scratches his head in bewilderment.

FIRST GUARD:

Where do you think he is?

SECOND GUARD (pointing off):

We better try those woods?

He walks away from the river, beating the brush. The other guard walks slowly after him looking here, there, and everywhere, absolutely stumped.[51]

DISSOLVE INTO:

179. HIGHWAY DUSK

James Allen comes out of the brush at the roadside. He sinks wearily down on a rock.

A Ford roadster comes around the curve in the distance. James Allen stares hard at it through the dusk, standing up now, ready to dive back into the brush. The car slows down as it approaches him. A young man is driving.

ALLEN:

Going into the city?

YOUNG MAN:

Hop in.

James Allen gets in. There is a box of peaches on the seat, and Allen has to hold them on his lap. The car starts on again.

180. INT. FORD

As the car goes along neither Allen nor the driver says anything. Allen watches him out of the corner of his eye, but the young man is intent on the road. James Allen looks down at the peaches, hungrily. The young man sees him staring at them.

YOUNG MAN:
Help yourself . . .

ALLEN:
Thanks.

He picks up a peach and starts to eat it, enjoying it. He stops in the middle of the second bite, staring down the road ahead at a car coming in the opposite direction.

181. TOURING CAR
loaded with men, bristling with guns.

182. INT. FORD
Allen keeps the peach and his hand up in front of his face as the other car approaches.

183. LONG SHOT
as the two cars pass each other.

184. INT. FORD

YOUNG MAN:
Wonder who they're after . . .

ALLEN:
Moonshiners—probably.

YOUNG MAN:
I'll find out tonight—my dad's the sheriff . . . over at Hillsboro.

Allen gives the boy a quick look, then turns and looks after the car. As it disappears in the distance Allen turns to look at the young man, watching his profile. The young man is just watching the road, showing no sign of suspicion.

DISSOLVE TO:

185. THE BROADWAY OF A LARGE SOUTHERN CITY
Bright lights, skyscrapers rising into the darkness, the streets thronged with people.

186. SIDEWALK

crowded with people out for an evening's entertainment. The CAMERA PICKS UP James Allen, very tired, but alert. A cop on the corner in the foreground. James Allen watches the cop. The cop turns toward Allen just as he reaches him. Allen looks quickly away and gets past all right.

187. CLOSE-UP TRUCKING

with James Allen, his face tense and strained.

DISSOLVE TO:

188. SCREEN FILLED WITH COPS

standing on corners, watching, another with back to CAMERA, others approaching, the face of an eagle-eyed copper coming bigger and bigger into the CAMERA.

DISSOLVE TO:

189. CLOSE-UP TRUCKING

James Allen's face, strained and drawn, with a hunted, haunted look. He stops and glances furtively around.

190. CHEAP HABERDASHERY

with a sign on the window: Cohen's Classy Clothes.[52]

DISSOLVE TO:

191. MIRROR

We see James Allen in a second-hand suit that doesn't fit very well. He still has his black prison hat on. He runs his hand over his heavy beard—with a shave he will look fairly respectable.

DISSOLVE TO:

192. INT. SMALL BARBERSHOP

Allen is lying in a barber's chair with his face covered with lather. In the background can be seen the front door of the barbershop and the street beyond, lit by streetlights. The barber finishes stropping the razor and commences to shave Allen.

BARBER:

How'd you get the scratches?

ALLEN:

Lumberjacking—up in the hills.

BARBER (with interest):

Is that a fact? I know a good many of them fellows up there. Funny I ain't seen you before.

ALLEN (pretending to be angry to change the subject):

Ouch! Say, watch it, will you?

BARBER:

Sorry.

There is the sound of the door opening and closing.

VOICE:

How are you, Bill?

The barber looks up. It is a cop, who is evidently in the habit of dropping in and who sits down sprawled out in a chair.

BARBER (looking up):

Well, if it ain't old John Law himself. (Allen stiffens perceptibly.) What's new—anything?

COP:

Yeah—there was a break on the Merritt County chain gang this morning. They think he's headed up this way.

BARBER (whistling):

What's the guy look like?

COP:

About five feet ten—stocky—thick black hair—brown eyes—somewhere around thirty . . . Name's Allen—James Allen . . .

The barber is shaving the last of the lather off Allen's face. Sweat has come out on Allen's forehead. He knows that in a minute the barber is going to sit him up face to face with the cop. His hands clench the arms of the chair desperately as he tries to keep his self-control. There is a tense silence while the barber shaves off the last of the lather.

ALLEN (quickly):

Give me a hot towel, will you?

BARBER:

Coming up . . . (He prepares the steaming towel and puts it over Allen's face.) Hope it's hot enough for you. (To cop.) Those guys haven't got much chance of getting away with it, have they?

COP:

No—we got the depot and all the highways out of town covered. They can get this far—and no farther.

The cop picks up the *Liberty* magazine and starts to run through it. The barber takes the towel off Allen's face. He sprinkles on some shaving lotion, wipes it off with a clean towel, and then powders Allen's face. Allen lies there tense and desperate. The barber pulls the chair up with a bang.

193. THE CEILING FROM ALLEN'S ANGLE

As the barber pulls the lever the CAMERA PANS DOWN the wall to CLOSE-UP of the policeman.[53]

194. CLOSE-UP OF ALLEN

Allen sees the cop for the first time.

195. FULL SHOT

The cop is reading the *Liberty*. Allen's prison hat hangs on a peg just over the cop's head. Allen gives the barber some money, watching the cop out of the corner of his eye.

BARBER:

Thanks. Come in again.

Allen steels himself and crosses to get his hat. He drops the hat and has to pick it up. The cop gives him a casual glance. Allen puts his hand over his face as though feeling the shave.

BARBER:

How was it—close enough?

ALLEN:

Plenty.

Allen goes out the door.[54]

196. EXT. BARBERSHOP

Allen starts up the street, increasing his pace as he gets out of sight of the shop.

197. MED. SHOT OF ALLEN

walking rapidly down the city street at night. He walks faster and faster, never looking behind. At the end of the block he turns a corner.

DISSOLVE TO:

198. MED. SHOT OF ALLEN NIGHT

walking down a less crowded street, still walking very fast. He hurries across the street and around the opposite corner, apparently trying to zigzag through the city.

DISSOLVE TO:

199. MED. SHOT OF ALLEN

walking down a street that is almost deserted, zigzagging across and around the opposite corner.

DISSOLVE TO:

200. MED. CLOSE-UP OF ALLEN

on a dark, completely deserted street. For the first time he slackens his pace, pauses, and looks around. He heaves a sigh of relief and wipes the sweat from his forehead. He sees a sign which reads

ROOMS 75¢ AND UP

He consults a piece of paper to see if he has the right number. He hesitates a moment, glances rapidly up and down the street, then enters the narrow doorway of the rooming house and starts upstairs.

201. INT. ROOMING HOUSE

shooting from halfway up the flight of stairs toward the open front door and the sidewalk beyond. Allen is walking up the stairs. Suddenly, footsteps are heard on the pavement. Allen flattens himself against the wall on the stairs and glances back toward the street. A policeman passes the doorway, swinging a club and whistling. As he advances Allen turns again to the stairs and continues mounting.[55]

202. INT. SECOND FLOOR OF ROOMING HOUSE

The room is dingy and fitted up as a cheap reception room. There is a hotel desk and switchboard on one side of the room, but at the moment there is no one there. Allen crosses to the desk, on which there is a bell. He touches the bell with the palm of his hand. It rings, but no one appears behind the desk. Suddenly a voice from outside the shot electrifies Allen.

VOICE:

So you hung it on the limb!

Allen recognizes the welcome voice of Barney and turns around.

203. DIFFERENT ANGLE

It is Barney. Happily, he puts his arm around Allen. They both grin.

ALLEN:

Barney!

BARNEY:

It's good to see you, kid!

ALLEN:

Same here . . . Got a place I can hide out?

BARNEY:

Sure . . . Come on. I'll fix you up.

Barney leads the way down a short hall and opens a door.

204. INT. BEDROOM

as Barney and Allen come in. Barney shuts the door.

ALLEN:

Think I'll be safe here tonight?

BARNEY:

You're a cinch—unless the cops pull another raid. (He grins at Allen's alarm.) Don't worry about that. They're probably too busy looking for *you* to raid any joints like this . . .

Allen sinks down on the bed exhausted.

ALLEN:

All I need is some sleep—I'll lam out of here early in the morning.

Barney is getting a bottle of whiskey out of a drawer. He pours a couple of drinks.

BARNEY (pouring drinks):

Well, make yourself at home—we got everything you dream about in the chain gang. (He hands a drink toward Allen.) Here—I guess you still know what this is good for . . .

ALLEN (refusing):

Thanks—I got a tough day ahead of me tomorrow.

BARNEY:

Well, I got a tough night ahead of *me*. (He gulps down his drink.) I got to beat it now, Jim—but the place is yours . . . (He moves over to the door.) Wait a minute—I'll get somebody to see that you're comfortable . . .

He steps over to the door and goes out. Allen starts to take off his coat. He looks around as he hears Barney come back in. Barney has a girl with him in flashy lounging pajamas, cut very low and very tight.

BARNEY:

This is Jim Allen, a pal of mine from the chain gang . . . He's just escaped.

ALLEN:

Listen—never mind the advertising.

BARNEY:

It's all right with Linda . . . (Then to Linda.) Take good care of him, babe—he's my personal guest. (To Allen.) So long, Jim. I hope you make it.

Barney ducks out. Linda sits down in a chair looking at Allen.

205. CLOSE-UP

Linda. She is pretty but there is a hard bitterness in her face. This expression melts somewhat as she looks at Allen. She admires him for his courage and is also attracted to him. As she sits there the close-fitting pajamas accentuate her sensuous body.

206. CLOSE-UP

Allen as he appraises her. This is his first contact alone with a woman for many years. She probably looks more tempting to him than if he had met her years ago, for he is sex-hungry. But he has the common sense to realize that he must try to concentrate all his thoughts on successfully concluding his escape. And therefore, in the first part of this scene, he is keeping himself well in hand.

207. WIDER ANGLE
taking in both. The girl catches Allen speculating about her. She smiles toward him invitingly, but he does not accept the hint. In fact, he averts his eyes from her.

LINDA (sincerely):
You've got plenty of what it takes—to pull an escape from *that* place.

ALLEN (sitting down wearily):
I'm not safe yet . . . Not until I'm out of the state.[56]

LINDA:
You'll make it . . .

This is a sincere hope that she states as a fact. Allen relaxes in the chair, resting his head contentedly on the back of the chair and looking up toward the ceiling.

ALLEN:
It's like a dream—being out . . . You don't know how I feel.

208. CLOSE-UP
Linda. An almost spiritual look comes into her worldly eyes.

LINDA:
Don't I? (There is a pause, a sigh; then.) Gee! To get away from a spot you hate . . . and forget it . . . and start all over again! (Looking at him with mingled emotions.) It takes nerve—I envy you . . . (Bitterly.) You're brave, all right!

209. WIDER ANGLE
taking in both.

ALLEN:

The brave one is the man who sticks there . . . *I* couldn't.

Linda rises, goes over to him, and sits on the arm of his chair.

LINDA (sincerely):

If there's anything I can do to help you, just say the word.

He looks up at her with a wonderful realization that in this rough diamond he has a true friend. Impulsively, he takes her hand and presses it.

ALLEN (warmly):

Thanks. (The contact of her hand in his stirs the man in him, and as he realizes it he quickly withdraws his hand, steeling himself.) But there's nothing you can do.

There is a pause. Linda looks down at him. She would like to stay there with him. He catches her looking at him, but Linda is unabashed.

LINDA:

How about a drink?

ALLEN:

Barney asked me, too—but I'm going to lay off.

LINDA:

Don't mind if I take one, do you?

ALLEN:

Go ahead.

As Linda gets up and pours herself a drink Allen finds himself looking at her with renewed interest. The sex urge will not be stifled.

210. CLOSE PAN SHOT

on Linda as if Allen's eyes were taking in every portion

of her body. The camera starts at her head and slowly passes the womanly curves of her breasts and hips. It pans down to her shapely legs and we hold it there.

211. CLOSE SHOT

taking in both. Linda is standing with the drink in her hand. Allen does not realize that he is staring at her now like a hungry animal. It does not disturb Linda. She raises the drink.

LINDA:

> Here's to you! A guy with your nerve has the breaks coming to him. (She takes the drink, then goes over to him again and sits on the arm of the chair while Allen still is in a sort of trance as he realizes that right now he craves this woman. When Allen doesn't speak she finally bridges the gap; she puts her hand on his arm.) Say—I know what you're thinking . . . I understand . . . You're among friends.[57]

Allen makes one last attempt to keep his feet on the ground.

ALLEN (huskily):

> I think you'd better clear out . . . I ought to get to sleep . . . I've got a heavy day ahead of me.

Linda looks at him admiringly.

LINDA (almost worshipfully):

> You're a gentleman, too . . . and there's not many of them left.

She picks up a package of cigarettes and offers one to Allen. He takes it. His hand is trembling. As he lights it this is particularly apparent. Linda has taken a cigarette for herself. Allen does not notice this and blows out his match.

LINDA:

Light mine, will you?

ALLEN:

Sorry.

He strikes another match and rises to light Linda's cigarette. Her face comes very close to his as he lights it. Their eyes meet and say more than any words possibly could. He wants her—now. And she knows it. He flings away the match and without a word hungrily crushes her in his arms. She makes no resistance as her body melts right into his. He starts to caress her wildly, his hand stroking her greedily. Their lips meet.

FADE OUT

FADE IN

212. INT. BEDROOM CLOSE-UP

Linda's hand removing the top from a coffee container.

DISSOLVE TO:

213. CLOSE-UP

Linda's hand on an open timetable, her finger pointing to "Booneville . . . 9:05." The coffee container, practically empty now, is in the shot. CAMERA PULLS BACK and we see Linda and Allen at the table.

LINDA:

Don't forget—the trolley to Booneville—and you can get the nine-o-five train north from there.

ALLEN:

I know my lesson. (As he puts on his coat.) And I better get started.

LINDA (pointing to some money that is on the table):

You're a sap not to take this money. (She looks at him pleadingly; she wants him to take it.)

ALLEN (choked with emotion):

I can't—from you.

LINDA:

Don't be a sucker—if you're going to get away you got to take every break you can . . . (She puts the money in the pocket of his coat.) You can send the money back to me sometime . . .

ALLEN:

I will—the first dough I get I'll mail you here . . .

LINDA (weary and bitter):

No hurry—I'll be at this address a long time—

ALLEN (taking her hand):

You've been so decent—I don't know what to say.

LINDA (simply):

Don't say anything!

She moves with him to the door. He looks at her, takes her in his arms, kisses her, and then he leaves without a word. She looks longingly after him.

DISSOLVE INTO:

214. STATION SIGN "BOONEVILLE"

DISSOLVE TO:

215. FULL SHOT

of the small-town station. James Allen is seen approaching the ticket window. There are a few people around the station.

216. TICKET WINDOW

as James Allen comes up and puts a ten-dollar bill through the window.

ALLEN:

Nashville on the nine-o-five.

CLERK (taking money):

Round trip?

ALLEN:

One way.

The clerk marks a ticket, stamps it, and hands it to Allen. He glances at schedule and clock.

CLERK:
The train's late. You've got thirty-five minutes.

James Allen looks around the station. Several of the natives are already looking casually at the stranger. He doesn't want to hang around the station thirty-five minutes and attract attention.

217. FULL SHOT STATION
Allen walks away from the ticket window and toward the main street of the town, which runs into the station.

DISSOLVE TO:

218. A HOT DOG WAGON
The station is seen in the near background. James Allen is drinking a bottle of Coke. There is a greasy proprietor attending. A hamburger is frying on the fire.

HOT DOG MAN:
You want everything on this one, too?

ALLEN:
Yeah—just like the first one—

James Allen stands watching toward the station.

CUT TO:

219. BOONEVILLE STATION
A horse-drawn buggy drives up and a man in a big Stetson alights. There is something very officious in his manner as he strides toward the tracks.

CUT TO:

220. HOT DOG WAGON
Allen is still looking toward the station. The hot dog man nods in that direction.

HOT DOG MAN:
Look who's here—the chief of police in all his glory!

He gives Allen the hamburger.

CUT TO:

221. BOONEVILLE STATION

Three other men join the chief of police.

CUT TO:

222. HOT DOG WAGON

James Allen and the hot dog man both looking toward the station.

HOT DOG MAN:

Must be looking for somebody important.

James Allen doesn't answer. He stands staring toward the station. A train whistle is heard from nearby.

HOT DOG MAN:

Well, we'll find out in a few minutes what all the doings is about.

223. BOONEVILLE STATION

The chief and his men stand watching as the train pulls in and stops.

CUT TO:

224. HOT DOG WAGON

James Allen watching, eating the hamburgers. He doesn't know what to do with the chief waiting there. He looks around slowly. There isn't anything else to do but to take a chance. He takes a last bite of the hamburger and starts toward the station.

225. CLOSE-UP

trucking with Allen as he goes toward the station. He walks along boldly, but his face is tense and strained. Suddenly

VOICE (from off-scene):

There he is![58]

Allen continues to walk along with a frozen face.

226. MED. SHOT

Allen is walking along as from another direction somebody points to a man, whereupon the chief and others start in hot pursuit as the man begins to run. They all whiz past Allen, who continues to walk in the other direction, outwardly calm.

227. TRUCK SHOT

as Allen continues to walk along toward the station with a frozen face.

228. REVERSE ANGLE

as the crowd pursues the wrong man, who dashes around to the opposite side of the train with the others still in pursuit.

229. JAMES ALLEN

Relieved, he walks across the station and gets on the last car of the train. Nobody pays any attention to him.

230. INT. RAILROAD CAR

James Allen sits down in the last seat.

DISSOLVE TO:

231. WHEELS OF ENGINE

starting to move.

DISSOLVE TO:

232. INT. CAR

James Allen sits like a statue, tense, motionless. If he gets away with this he is well on his way to freedom. The conductor glances into the last car. His face shows his surprise at seeing anyone in the car. He advances on James Allen, eyeing him suspiciously.

CONDUCTOR:

Did I get your ticket?

ALLEN:

Here it is. (Hands him ticket.)

CONDUCTOR (looking at ticket):
Booneville, eh? You must have got on without my seeing you—

ALLEN:
They were chasing somebody— I guess you were watching—

CONDUCTOR (eyeing Allen):
They were after an escaped convict—

ALLEN (casually):
Catch him?

CONDUCTOR:
No—the guy they caught turned out to be a hobo. (He punches the ticket and looks hard at Allen.) They're still looking for the convict.

Allen takes the ticket and puts it back in his pocket. The conductor turns away and starts up the car. James Allen looks after him. At the platform doorway the conductor meets the brakeman. They stand there, talking in undertones that we do not hear above the rattle of the train, casting puzzled glances at James Allen. Allen sits looking out the window. Finally the two trainmen turn away.

233. CLOSE-UP
James Allen watches them go, relieved again.

DISSOLVE TO:

234. TRAIN WHEELS
clicking off the miles.

DISSOLVE TO:

235. INT. DAY COACH MED. CLOSE-UP OF JAMES ALLEN
seated next to the window. Facing him is a talkative traveling salesman, puffing on a big cigar. Beside the salesman and in plain view is a small black bag of the sort salesmen use to carry samples in.

SALESMAN (who has obviously been talking for some time):

You can't get around the fact that traveling broadens you. I figure I've covered over twenty thousand miles in the last year—

ALLEN:

What do you sell?

SALESMAN:

Rubber bands—sink stoppers—hot water bottles— (Taking out a card and handing it to Allen.) C. K. Hobbs is the name— (He pauses and glances at Allen, sizing him up.) You look like a guy that's been places.

ALLEN:

Yeah. (He slips the card into his pocket.)

SALESMAN:

It's the only life. When I can't hit the road I'm licked.

ALLEN (grimly):

Me too.

SALESMAN:

Excitement—change—running for trains and missing 'em— They'll tell you there's no such thing as adventure anymore, but I know different. (Handing Allen a newspaper.) Read this, for instance.

Allen takes the newspaper.

INSERT of the newspaper. Its lead story tells about Allen's escape and the hunt that is being made to find him.

BACK TO SCENE:
as Allen tries to be calm as he glances over the paper.

SALESMAN:

Now there's adventure for you! Ten to one they'll get him. They'll be watching for him at Nashville—

and all points out of the state—but if I were that guy—boy! I'd give 'em a chase.

ALLEN:
What would you do?

SALESMAN:
Well—that depends. You gotta lose your identity, for one thing.

ALLEN:
Disguise, you mean?

SALESMAN (with a tolerant laugh):
That's too much bother. It doesn't matter how much you look like yourself so long as you can prove you're someone else. For instance—so far as you're concerned, I'm C. K. Hobbs of Philadelphia, a salesman of standard rubber goods. Have you any way of knowing that I'm not? (He glances at Allen.)

ALLEN (shaking his head):
No.

SALESMAN (triumphantly):
Well—there you are. Think that over. (He smiles mysteriously.)

At this moment a pretty blonde comes walking down the aisle. She glances at Allen and the salesman. She smiles slightly, passes on to the rear of the car, and goes out on the platform to get some air. The salesman's eyes have followed her. He observes that the girl is alone on the platform outside and turns to Allen.

SALESMAN:
I think I see a prospect.

He gets up and starts down the corridor after the girl.

CUT TO:

236. SMALL-TOWN STATION PLATFORM

showing the train pull in and come to a stop. The name of the town, Munro, is in evidence. There are quite a few people on the platform, getting on and off the train. In the foreground are three plainclothesmen, a sheriff, and two or three policemen. Presently Allen is seen descending from the train with the salesman's little black bag in his hand. The sheriff, the policemen, and the plainclothesmen intercept Allen.

SHERIFF:

Wait a minute there—we want to have a little talk with you.

Allen stops, pretending surprise.

ALLEN:

With me?

SHERIFF:

Yeah, with you. What's your name?

ALLEN:

C. K. Hobbs—rubber goods salesman. (He hands him Hobbs's card.)

SHERIFF:

Yeah? Let's take a look in that bag.

Allen hands the bag to the sheriff. The sheriff opens it and draws out a hot water bottle. Several people standing around laugh.

SHERIFF:

All right. No hard feelings, I hope, Mr. Hobbs. We're after an escaped convict—and we got to do our duty.

ALLEN:

That's all right. Selling hot water bottles is pretty dull—a little excitement doesn't come in bad.

SHERIFF:

Say, let's see that hot water bottle again. (Allen hands him the hot water bottle.) How much for this one?

ALLEN:

I'm not supposed to sell those samples—but just to show there aren't any hard feelings I'll let you have that one for three dollars.

SHERIFF (shelling out three bucks):

Thanks—I hope I'll be able to do a favor for you some day, Mr. Hobbs. So long—

ALLEN:

So long—

Allen shuts up the black sample case and starts away. The sheriff stands admiring the hot water bottle.

DISSOLVE TO:

237. COUNTY HIGHWAY

showing James Allen trudging along. The tenseness of the chase is now gone. His stride is relaxed and easy. The country is attractive and the weather good.

DISSOLVE TO:

238. ALLEN'S FEET TREADING THE HIGHWAY

DISSOLVE TO:

239. WHEELS OF A MOVING AUTOMOBILE

DISSOLVE TO:

240. WHEELS OF A SPEEDING TRAIN

FADE OUT

FADE IN

241. ON A CROWDED STREET IN CHICAGO

showing Allen approaching the policeman standing on a corner in the foreground. Allen holds up a newspaper to the policeman and points to an item.

INSERT NEWSPAPER AD

MAN WANTED
General work. $20. Wk.
615 So. Main Street

BACK TO SCENE:

The policeman points with his club.

POLICEMAN:

Next corner—turn to your left. It's two blocks down.

ALLEN:

Thanks.

DISSOLVE TO:

242. EXT. WINDOW OF A PASTRY SHOP

In one corner of the window is a cardboard sign: Man Wanted—General Work. James Allen enters the shot. Just as he does so, the hand of an employee reaches in the window and removes the sign, indicating that the position has been filled. Allen pauses, glances hungrily into the window laden with pastry, shrugs his shoulders, and walks on down the street.[59]

FADE OUT

FADE IN

243. CLOSE-UP OF DOOR

On it is the following lettering:

TRI-STATE ENGINEERING CO.
Labor Personnel Office

DISSOLVE TO:

244. INT. PERSONNEL OFFICE

Allen is standing at the desk of the personnel manager.

PERSONNEL MANAGER:

I guess we can use you . . . What's the name?

He picks up a pen to fill out an employment card.

ALLEN (before he realizes what he is saying):

Allen . . .

The manager starts to write; then he pauses.

PERSONNEL MANAGER:
Is that the first or last name?

ALLEN (realizing he had better be careful):
First name . . . My full name's Allen James.

The manager writes the name on the card.

DISSOLVE INTO:

INSERT of a time card of the Tri-State Engineering Co. It is dated 1924, contains the name of Allen James and the fact that he is employed as a laborer at a wage of four dollars per day.

DISSOLVE INTO:

245. A PICK
as it is swung down and bites into the ground several times. CAMERA DRAWS BACK, revealing Allen working with a road gang—no chains, no guards. The men stop, stretch, mop their brows, and joke at leisure. Allen pauses to wipe the sweat off his forehead.[60] The foreman steps up to him.

FOREMAN:
Say, James—that was a swell idea you had about the bend up there.

ALLEN:
Thanks.

FOREMAN:
I told the boss you suggested it— (slapping him on the back) and I don't think you'll be swinging a pick much longer.

Allen smiles appreciatively.

DISSOLVE INTO:

INSERT of another time card of the Tri-State Engineering Co. The date is now 1925, and Allen James is an assistant foreman at a wage of six dollars per day.

DISSOLVE INTO:

246. INT. BOARDINGHOUSE ROOM

It is a rather nice room. Marie and Allen have just come in. She is twenty-six, dark, and sexy looking. She is the kind of a girl that must have her man. Allen is inspecting the room as she talks. He is paying but little attention to her, but she is eyeing him critically, and she likes him.

MARIE (as they enter):
This is the room that's for rent.

ALLEN:
It's mighty nice . . . What are you asking for it?

MARIE:
Twenty-five a month—and that's very reasonable.

ALLEN:
Very—but it's more than I feel I can pay . . . I'm sorry—because I like the location . . . It's not far from the bridge I'm working on—

MARIE:
I'm sorry, too . . . (with a tone that is not all business) because I'd like to rent this room to a gentleman like yourself.

ALLEN (lightly; with a chuckle):
But you don't know anything about me . . .

MARIE (with a meaning smile):
Oh, I can tell . . . You look like you'd be sociable . . . and friendly . . . not like a stranger around the house. (He smiles back appreciatively. If he gets her inner meaning he does not show it.) How much would you be willing to pay?

ALLEN:
Really—it's out of the question.

MARIE (quickly):
Suppose I made it *twenty* dollars . . .

She looks at him anxiously, hoping he will say yes.

ALLEN (trying to be fair and not entirely sensing that Marie is more anxious to have him than the matter of how much she will get for the room):

That's silly . . . You can easily get your price for it.

He shakes his head that he had better not consider it.

MARIE:

Well—I'm willing to let it go for twenty . . . (looking at him with her big eyes) to you.

Allen considers.

DISSOLVE INTO:

INSERT of another time card of the Tri-State Engineering Co. The date is now 1926, and Allen James is a foreman at a wage of nine dollars per day.

DISSOLVE INTO:

247. INT. BOARDINGHOUSE ROOM

starting with a CLOSE-UP of a book entitled *Civil Engineering*. As the CAMERA BACKS AWAY there is Allen seated in a comfortable chair reading the book. As the CAMERA takes in still more of the room we see that Marie is standing near the door. Allen is not aware she is there and keeps on pouring over the book. She is dressed in a most unconventional negligee. She looks at Allen and shakes her head impatiently. She is undoubtedly annoyed at him. But she stifles her feelings and says over-pleasantly:

MARIE:

Hello, honey . . .

ALLEN (without glancing up from his book):

Hello . . .

This gets Marie sore. She makes no attempt now to hide her burned-up feelings.

MARIE (hard):
All you do every night is *study* . . .

ALLEN (looking up just long enough to answer her):
I won't get anywhere if I don't . . . Anyway, that's not true . . . We were out last night.

Marie sighs. She crosses toward him and tries to be kittenish.

MARIE:
I don't think you like me anymore.

Allen impatiently slams his book shut. This kitten stuff annoys him.

ALLEN:
Of course I do . . . but we can't always be playing around . . . Anyway, what's that got to do with it?

MARIE (putting her arm around him; he does not like it but he allows her to do it):
Well—I don't know—but— (She can't resist putting in the sting.) You don't act like you used to . . . now I don't seem good enough for you.

ALLEN:
You're imagining things.

MARIE:
No—I'm not. (Her whimpering does not ring sincere.) When you were first here, you weren't this way . . . You've grown tired of me . . . and I was silly enough to believe you—when you said you loved me.

Allen looks up at her provoked. He rises.

ALLEN:
I said I *loved* you? (Softly but forcibly.) Now, Marie—you're trying to put me in a spot. I never said that . . . (emphatically) and you know it wasn't love—just as well as I do.

The truth hurts her. Allen looks her in the eye; she averts his look for a moment, then turns back to him with the expression of a tigress in her face.

MARIE:

So that's how you feel! You can't make me out cheap and get away with it! I know what I'm talking about—and some day you're going to be sorry!

She turns and leaves the room rapidly, slamming the door after her. Allen gazes at the door, frowning; then he turns back to his book.

DISSOLVE INTO:

INSERT of another time card of the Tri-State Engineering Co. This one is dated 1927. The wage is up to twelve dollars. Allen James is a surveyor.[61]

DISSOLVE INTO:

248. EXT. ROAD IN THE HILLS

James Allen, in surveyor's clothes, is standing talking to another man. They hold a blueprint between them.

ALLEN (pointing with his finger):

We bring it down around there—across here—and that's it. Understand?

ASSISTANT:

Yes, sir. (As a car drives up. Allen sees the car.)

ALLEN:

All right—go to it. I want to talk to the superintendent.

A man in street clothes is getting out of the car. Allen goes up to him.

MARKWELL (excitedly):

Say, James—I saw a lot of equipment down there ready to cut through Altar Hill . . .

ALLEN:

Yes . . . I had it sent down there.

MARKWELL:

That way will cost twice as much. It would even be cheaper to put the road through Blake's land and pay the outrageous price he's asking . . .

ALLEN:

I know that . . . But Blake doesn't.

MARKWELL:

What do you mean?

ALLEN:

Blake saw that equipment down at the hill too . . . (Allen grins.) He wants to talk to you—his price isn't so outrageous now . . .

DISSOLVE INTO:

INSERT of another time card of the Tri-State Engineering Co. This one is dated 1929. Allen James is an assistant superintendent and his wage is fourteen dollars per day.

DISSOLVE INTO:

249. INT. ALLEN'S ROOM IN BOARDINGHOUSE

Allen is packing a suitcase. There is a knock on the door and Marie enters immediately.

MARIE:

So you really think you're leaving . . .

ALLEN:

I want a bigger place . . . and I can afford it now.

MARIE (sitting):

I suppose you're leaving *me* for good, too.

ALLEN (continues packing):

No . . . we'll probably see each other sometimes.

MARIE:

You don't mean that . . .

ALLEN (stops packing):

Listen, Marie—I appreciate all you've done for me.

But I couldn't fall in love with you—you just didn't get me that way . . .

MARIE (interrupting him):

And that's the only reason?

ALLEN:

It's a pretty good one, isn't it?

MARIE:

Not very. Of course . . . when a fellow wants to ditch a girl, he'll do most anything . . . providing it doesn't land him back in a *chain gang*—where he probably belongs.

250. CLOSE-UP

of Allen. He whirls around, staring at her, speechless.

251. CLOSE-UP

of Marie. She remains very cool. She takes a letter from her dress and hands it to Allen.

MARIE:

It's from your brother.

252. CLOSE-UP

of Allen. He mechanically takes the letter. He stares dully at it. His face blanches.

INSERT of a letter from Allen's brother. We IRIS on this particular part of it:

> . . . and I thought that you ought to know that the police are still trying to find you. When I think that your capture would mean eight more terrible years on that chain gang, my blood runs cold . . .

BACK TO SCENE:

Allen looks up from the letter horrified, terrified.

253. CLOSE SHOT
Allen and Marie.

ALLEN (looking up at her, terrified):
Marie—you—you wouldn't tell . . .

MARIE:
Not if I had a reason to protect you.

ALLEN:
What do you mean?

MARIE:
I wouldn't tell—if you were my husband.

Allen stares at her for a moment, then down at the letter. He looks up at her again, trapped. She knows she has won.

DISSOLVE INTO:

INSERT of a marriage license. It bears the names of Allen James and Marie Edwards. We see the year 1929.

DISSOLVE INTO:

254. CLOSE-UP OF A DOOR
It is lettered as follows:

MR. ALLEN JAMES
General Field Superintendent
Private

DISSOLVE INTO:

255. INT. ALLEN'S OFFICE
MODEL OF CONCRETE BRIDGE on his desk. CAMERA PULLS BACK and we see Allen at his desk with Fuller, one of his assistants. Both are studying the model.

FULLER:
It means plenty of work . . .

ALLEN:
I'm used to that . . .

FULLER:

Yes—but, on the other hand, all work and no play—

ALLEN (laughing):

Makes "jack."

FULLER:

But you ought to knock off for a little recreation . . . My wife and I are giving a little party at the Club Chateau tonight. How about joining us?

ALLEN:

I'd really like to.

FULLER:

Fine—and that includes *Mrs.* James.

ALLEN (hesitating):

I'm not sure she can come—but I'll ask her.

FULLER:

Well—anyway—we'll expect *you*.

Fuller exits. Allen consults some papers on his desk. The door opens. His secretary enters; she puts some more papers before him.

SECRETARY:

This is the revised budget on the King's Highway Bridge. (Allen nods.) And while you were out, your wife called.

ALLEN (uninterested):

Any message?

SECRETARY:

She said she won't be home until Wednesday—she left with her cousin for the country.

ALLEN (dully):

I see . . .

SECRETARY:
She also said her account's overdrawn by about six hundred dollars.

Allen is stunned and angry.

ALLEN (annoyed greatly):
She's got to stop it . . . The same thing happened last month. (Then realizing the presence of his secretary, he sighs resignedly.) All right—make out a check for whatever it is—and deposit it when you go to lunch.

As the secretary exits he angrily picks up some papers on his desk and rattles them unnecessarily to give vent to the mood that his wife has thrown him into.

FADE OUT

FADE IN

256. INT. CLUB CHATEAU
The Fuller party is at a large table in the foreground—a gay set who have been drinking, but none of them are really tight. Allen is in the party. Near him sits a girl whom we will find as Helen. Allen has not quite caught the spirit of revelry. Now the orchestra starts a number and, in ad libs which cannot be distinctly heard by us, different gentlemen in the party invite various ladies to dance, until Allen and Helen are the only ones left at the table.

257. FULL SHOT
as the couples dance. The floor is very crowded.

258. CLOSE SHOT
Allen and Helen. She sits several seats removed from him. She smiles at him. He gets up and takes a seat beside her.

HELEN:
Don't you dance?

ALLEN:
Not if I can get out of it.

His frankness pleases the girl. In fact, she seems relieved to know that she does not have to dance.

HELEN:
That makes two of us . . . At least, I don't like dancing on such a crowded floor.

ALLEN:
I don't like crowds anywhere.[62]

HELEN:
Again we agree. (A pause. Allen looks at her and there is no doubt that she appeals to him. She seems to like him, too. Finally—) I rather suspect this party bores you.

ALLEN:
It did . . . until now.

He smiles at her and she mocks a little curtsy.

HELEN:
That was a pretty speech.

ALLEN:
And one pretty speech deserves another . . . You should have said: "Likewise!"

HELEN (after a pause):
Well—I *was* on the verge of sneaking home . . . *Now* I'm not so sure I want to.

Though this is said lightly there is an undercurrent of sincerity. These two are talking like old friends.

ALLEN:
Thanks. (Leaning over toward her like a naughty kid as he suggests.) I don't think they'd miss us if we both made a getaway. (She pretends to be

shocked at the idea but ends her pretense with a merry twinkle in her eyes.) How about it?

HELEN (feigning indecision):
Well . . .

She starts to get up. He is pleased as he also rises.

DISSOLVE INTO:

259. EXT. LAKE DRIVE MOVING SHOT NIGHT

moving along with Allen and Helen as he drives his roadster and she sits rather near him. Both seem at peace with the world.

HELEN:
Tell me more about your work. It's wonderfully fascinating.

ALLEN (with a twinkle in his eye):
Why talk about work?

HELEN (she knows she interests him and likes the idea; however, it is fun to fence):
Well—that's what interests you, isn't it?

ALLEN (looking at her admiringly):
Oh—other things interest me, too.

He looks into her eyes. She likes the implication but does not answer. There is a pause. He stops the car.

ALLEN (as he stops the car):
What about stopping here awhile—or must you go home?

HELEN:
There are no "musts" in my life. I'm free, white, and twenty-one.

ALLEN:
You're lucky.

HELEN:
Why?

ALLEN:

Well—you can go where you want—when you want—

HELEN (simply):

Can't you?

ALLEN (evasively):

Yes—and no.

Helen looks at him and seems to be able to read him rather accurately. She wants to help this man who she feels is in need of sympathy and understanding.

HELEN:

You're a strange, moody person . . . You need someone to pull you out of the doldrums.

ALLEN:

Maybe. (More lightly.) Are you applying for the job?

HELEN (in a light vein):

I might consider it.

ALLEN (enjoying the game):

You're hired.

HELEN:

When do I start?

ALLEN (looking at her meaningly):

You started—several hours ago.

They look at each other amusedly, but their expressions become more serious as we

FADE OUT

FADE IN

260. BRIDGE LONG SHOT

under construction. This bridge is the materialization of the model bridge which was in Allen's office. The day is balmy and bright. The location is idyllic. Helen is walking and stops at a tree to watch the construction of the bridge. Allen has been giving some instructions to the men. Now he sees her.

261. CLOSE SHOT

of Allen as he looks toward her with surprise and pleasure. He starts toward her.

262. CLOSE SHOT

Allen and Helen. Allen comes into the scene and takes her hand in a cordial greeting, holding it for a considerable portion of the scene.

HELEN:

Surprised to see me?

ALLEN:

I surely am. What brings you here?

HELEN (looking at him warmly):

You . . . I wanted to see you in action.

ALLEN (pleased that she is that interested):

That's nice—but there's nothing much to see here.

HELEN (surprised):

Nothing? I think it's awfully interesting . . . And such tremendous work! (Looking proudly at him.) You can't fool me—you're proud of it.

Allen tries to be nonchalant, but as she looks at him he cannot help but grin.

ALLEN (admittedly):

Well, I guess I am.

HELEN (loyally and sincerely):

You should be.

DISSOLVE INTO:

263. EXT. LAKE SHORE

Allen's roadster is parked at the same place where we

saw them in a previous sequence. They are looking out over the moonlit lake.

ALLEN:
This is a favorite spot of ours, isn't it?

HELEN (looking out over the water contentedly):
We're so alone here—I like it.

ALLEN:
So do I.

HELEN:
Remember the first time we came here—when I accepted that job? (Allen nods.) But I don't think I've succeeded. (Concernedly.) You're still in those doldrums—

ALLEN:
That's because there's lots of things I'd like to tell you—but I can't.

A pause. She looks at him. She takes his hand.

HELEN:
Why don't you?

ALLEN (fervently as he puts his hand on hers):
I'd like to—because I need you—and want you . . . You know I love you, Helen— (Restraining himself from crushing her in his arms.) But first—I've got to be—*free!*

He continues to press her hand with pent-up emotion. She looks at him lovingly. Her eyes plead with him to tell her more.[63]

FADE OUT

FADE IN

264. INT. APARTMENT HALLWAY CLOSE-UP
of Allen at the door of his apartment. On the door is a card: Mr. and Mrs. James Allen [*sic*]. It is a high-class

apartment house. Allen takes a key from his pocket, unlocks the door, and goes in.

CUT TO:

265. INT. ALLEN'S LIVING ROOM

as Allen comes in. The room is beautifully furnished but in utter disorder. He looks on the end table which is littered with cigarette butts. Several empty cocktail glasses are also on it. On another table he sees a number of empty gin bottles. He shakes his head, annoyed. He starts to try to clean up the place when the telephone rings. He goes over to the phone, takes the receiver from the hook.

ALLEN (in phone):

Hello . . .

CUT TO:

266. INT. TELEPHONE BOOTH

Sammy, a drunk, is reeling on his pins as he stands at a pay phone. He talks thickly. His tongue gets twisted occasionally.

SAMMY:

Hello, yourshelf . . . Marie there . . . ? Thash funny . . . Well, where do you think she is . . . ? She had a date with me—and she's giving me a shtandup. (Maudlin.) First dame who ever gave me a shtandup . . . Well, you can tell her that Sammy called—and you can tell her where she can go . . . with little Sammy's compliments. (Confidentially.) And listen, Mishter—not a word to her husband, understand?

He hangs up the phone and starts to reel away from it.

CUT TO:

267. INT. ALLEN'S LIVING ROOM

as Allen bangs up the receiver, angry as hell. He is disgusted, and he lets out his disgust on the gin bottles and glasses as he tries to make the room more livable. He looks at the clock.

268. CLOSE-UP OF CLOCK
It is almost midnight.

DISSOLVE INTO:

269. CLOSE-UP OF CLOCK
It is 2:15. We TRUCK BACK and find Marie is there. She is sitting in a chair. She looks slovenly and much the worse for wear after a hard night. Allen is pacing the floor. They are evidently in the midst of a conversation. He stops near her chair. Marie appears bored. Allen is tense.

ALLEN (desperately):
Don't you understand, Marie? I'm asking you for my freedom—real freedom. (Pleadingly.) If you get a divorce I'll give you anything you want . . . I swear I will.

MARIE (as she stamps out a cigarette on the floor):
What's the use of arguing—arguing—arguing?! I've told you I'm satisfied with things the way they are.

ALLEN:
Can't you see—neither of us can be happy this way?

Marie shrugs her shoulders.

MARIE:
I'm happy—and I'm taking no chances of letting you go.

ALLEN (disgustedly):
But what can I mean to you?

MARIE:
Listen, you're going to be a big shot someday—with plenty of sugar—and I'm going to ride right along

. . . get that? (Lighting cigarette.) I'm no fool . . . I'd be a sucker to let you out now.

ALLEN:
But I'm in love—don't you understand?

MARIE (puffing out some smoke):
That's just too bad.

ALLEN (unrelenting):
Why don't you play the game square?

270. CLOSE-UP MARIE
with a snarl.

MARIE:
So that you and your sweet mama can give me the grand go-by? (Waving him away with her hand.) Be yourself.

271. CLOSE-UP ALLEN
It is all he can do not to strangle her.

ALLEN (wildly):
If you won't listen to reason, I'll find some way!

272. CLOSE SHOT OF THE TWO
He looks at her menacingly. She rises in hot anger.

MARIE:
If you do, you'll serve out your time—and I mean it!

ALLEN (angrily):
It's no worse than serving out my life with you!

MARIE:
You'll be sorry you said that!

She starts away. He grabs her by the arm and wheels her around. He continues to hold her like a vise as he shouts at her.

ALLEN:

Listen! You've held a sword over my head long enough . . . And it's time we called quits . . . You've been pulling a bluff on me—and I've been coward enough to fall for it!

Marie tears herself from him.

MARIE:

You filthy, good-for-nothing convict! (Angrily.) A bluff, huh? (Sinisterly.) You'll see.

273. WIDER ANGLE

as she dashes for the phone and picks up the receiver.

ALLEN:

Put that down!

MARIE (into phone):

Hello . . . Give me the police station—anyone—I don't care.

Allen dashes across the room and grabs the phone from her hand. He throws her away from the telephone.

MARIE (wildly):

Do you think that'll stop me? Not when I've made up my mind.

She turns and dashes out of the room.

ALLEN (in a daze):

Marie!

He looks toward the door in a stupor. He is frightened.

FADE OUT

FADE IN

274. INT. ALLEN'S OFFICE

James Allen is seated at his desk. Three businessmen are seated around the room.

BUSINESSMAN:

We'll only take a minute of your time, Mr. James . . . In view of your marvelous achievement on the new Stevens bridge, the chamber of commerce would like you as their principal speaker at their next banquet.

A buzzer sounds as Allen is about to answer the men.

ALLEN:

One moment, please . . . (He switches a button and picks up the receiver of the dictograph.) Yes?

CUT TO:

275. GIRL AT DESK IN OUTER OFFICE

GIRL (into dictograph):

There are two detectives coming through, Mr. Allen [*sic*]. I told them you were busy, but they wouldn't wait.

CUT TO:

276. INT. ALLEN'S OFFICE

He lays the receiver down, in a daze, and rises slowly.

ALLEN (to chamber of commerce committee):

Gentlemen—I'll have to ask you to excuse me—

He is interrupted by the opening of the door. Two detectives enter unceremoniously.

FIRST DETECTIVE (to Allen):

We have a warrant here, *Mr. James*—or *Mr. Allen*—for your arrest.

Everyone is surprised. Allen is speechless.

FADE OUT

FADE IN

277. INT. WAITING ROOM

A uniformed guard shows James Allen in.

GUARD:

The district attorney says you can have as long as you like, Mr. Allen.

Allen nods his thanks. The guard crosses to another door and holds it open. As Helen comes in the guard closes the door from the outside.

For a moment Allen and Helen stand looking at each other silently, Allen's face ashamed and wondering how she is going to take it. Helen's face questioning.

HELEN (after a moment):

Is it true, Jimmie? (He nods.) How did they find out?

ALLEN:

My wife.

HELEN (unhappily):

It's so hard to believe it's true—you—*you*—

278. CLOSE-UP OF HELEN

She walks over to the window, looks out, then turns.

HELEN:

I don't even blame you for not telling me what you'd been— That wasn't you—*you're* a different person—you've made yourself into a new man. I love that new man—and I'm going to stick with him. (She crosses to him.)

279. WIDER ANGLE

ALLEN:

That gives me something to fight for, Helen.

HELEN:

You're going to win your fight, too— (She goes into his arms.) I'm for you, dear—*everybody's* for you—

DISSOLVE TO:

280. CHAMBER OF COMMERCE BANQUET ROOM CLOSE-UP OF CHAIRMAN
addressing the banquet, which we see as the CAMERA PULLS BACK.

CHAIRMAN:
—and that speaker, gentlemen, whose enforced absence from our banquet tonight has created nationwide indignation, is in need of our help. By hard work, diligence, and honesty he has risen to success and to a position of prominence and respect. He is now facing not only penal servitude, but actual slavery—barbarism—torture—for a crime he has already expiated many times before—a fugitive—not from justice but from injustice! In my opinion it is monstrous—and, as chairman of this chamber of commerce, I call upon you to pledge your unanimous support to James Allen—reputable engineer of this city, veteran of the World War, and citizen of the United States of America.

The people rise to their feet, cheering.[64]

DISSOLVE TO:

281. INT. PRISON CELL
Allen is in the cell. A lot of newspapermen are gathered there.

FIRST REPORTER (to Allen):
. . . And we can quote you literally?

ALLEN:
Certainly. Everything I've said are facts . . . I want this rotten chain gang system exposed . . . Print it all.

This pleases the reporters.

SECOND REPORTER (to Allen):
How about a special signed story from you for our Sunday supplement?

ALLEN (grimly):
I'll write it—gladly.

DISSOLVE TO:

INSERT of a Chicago newspaper with the following scarehead:

CHICAGO FIGHTS TO KEEP
ALLEN FROM CHAIN GANG

There is a news story under the head. There is also a large photograph of James Allen. SUPERIMPOSED on this photograph is a pencil sketch of "Blind Justice."

DISSOLVE TO:

INSERT of another newspaper. We shoot this so that we do not see in what city it is published. The headline reads:

LOCAL CHAIN GANG OFFICIALS INCENSED
OVER CHICAGO'S REFUSAL TO AID

There is a picture of James Allen. Over it is the caption "We want him back!"

DISSOLVE TO:

INSERT of a Chicago newspaper editorial page, IRISING on an editorial captioned:

IS THIS CIVILIZATION?

We can also read the first paragraph as follows:

> Shall we stand by while a man who has become a leading citizen of this city has the shadow of medieval torture creeping over him?

DISSOLVE INTO:

INSERT of the editorial page of a southern paper, IRISED on a particular editorial captioned:

STATE'S RIGHTS
WHAT HAS BECOME OF THEM?

The editorial goes on as follows:

> It is a sad state of affairs when the governor of one state refuses to recognize the rights of another.

FADE OUT

FADE IN

282. INT. DISTRICT ATTORNEY'S OFFICE CLOSE-UP JAMES ALLEN
as he sits in the district attorney's office.

DISTRICT ATTORNEY'S VOICE:
Governor Badger has not yet signed the extradition papers.

CAMERA PULLS BACK showing the district attorney, seated at his desk. Seated around are Allen, his attorney, and two representatives of the other state.

DISTRICT ATTORNEY (to representatives):
Until he does, I cannot turn Mr. Allen over to the custody of your state.

FIRST REPRESENTATIVE:
In view of Allen's record here since his escape, our state has authorized us to assure you that if he returns voluntarily and pays the expenses the state has been put to, he will be pardoned within ninety days.

ALLEN'S ATTORNEY:
But why is it necessary for my client to return at all? Why mete out punishment to a man who has proven himself a useful and honorable citizen?

FIRST REPRESENTATIVE:
Merely a technicality—no prisoner is eligible for pardon until he has served ninety days.

ALLEN:
You mean I'll have to serve ninety days—on the chain gang?

FIRST REPRESENTATIVE:
No—you will be given some clerical job in one of the camps.

ATTORNEY:
The matter rests entirely with my client—but I'd advise him to stay right here.

ALLEN (to D.A.):
There's someone else I'd like to consult. (He nods toward the door.) Will you excuse me a minute?

DISTRICT ATTORNEY:
Certainly.

Allen crosses to the door.

CUT TO:

283. EXT. ANTEROOM
Helen is seated in a chair. The door opens and Allen enters. She rises, looking at him questioningly.

ALLEN:
They've promised me a full pardon within ninety days if I go back.

HELEN (hesitatingly):
Can you trust them?

ALLEN:
I don't see why not! (Nods; then decisively.) Besides, I want to get it all cleaned up now—so nothing's hanging over our happiness.

HELEN:
It's best, dear . . . They can't fail to pardon you—when you deserve it so much. You'll be back in three months—free—for always— (She goes into his arms.) And we'll be together—for always—

CUT TO:

284. INT. DISTRICT ATTORNEY'S OFFICE
The men are waiting.

FIRST REPRESENTATIVE:
These stories you've been hearing are absurd, gentlemen. On the whole, our chain gangs are bene-

ficial to the convicts—not only physically, but morally—

He is interrupted by Allen's entrance from the other room.

ALLEN:
I'm going back with you—on your assurance of pardon.

FIRST REPRESENTATIVE (warmly):
And you won't regret your decision.

FADE OUT

FADE IN

285. ON A RAILROAD STATION

The train has just come to a stop and passengers are getting off. Reporters, photographers, and a crushing crowd are gathered about waiting for Allen.

Allen and the two representatives step off the train. Pictures are snapped. Reporters clamor for statements. William Ramsey steps up to Allen.[65]

286. CLOSE-UP OF ALLEN AND RAMSEY

RAMSEY:
My name is Ramsey.

ALLEN (shaking hands):
Oh—my attorney. Where do we go?

RAMSEY:
We'll go over to my office and get the financial end of this straightened out first.

They start to leave.

DISSOLVE TO:

287. INT. RAMSEY'S OFFICE

Ramsey sits at his desk. Allen is seated across from him, with pen and checkbook.

RAMSEY:

Your capture and return cost the state three hundred and fifty dollars . . . (Allen starts writing a check.) My fee will be twenty-five hundred—one thousand now and fifteen hundred on your release . . .

ALLEN (handing him first check):

That's for the state . . .

RAMSEY:

You know, of course, that you'll have to go to a prison camp for ninety days . . .

Allen nods and writes out another check.

ALLEN (handing him the check):

There's *your* check . . .

RAMSEY:

Thanks, Allen . . . (He blows on the check softly to dry it.)

ALLEN:

After those ninety days, there's no reason to believe I won't get my pardon then, is there?

RAMSEY:

Well—this is a funny state—and the governor's a little—er—peculiar. (Allen is puzzled.) You see—all that publicity you gave out about conditions here didn't help any.

ALLEN (troubled):

But I'll get the pardon?

RAMSEY (with lukewarm assurance only):

Oh—they'll give you the pardon—but that clerical job they promised you isn't definite . . . they might want you to work for about sixty days . . .

Allen frowns, worried.

FADE OUT

FADE IN

288. CLOSE-UP OF A BLACKBOARD

on which is written in chalk

TUTTLE COUNTY PRISON CAMP

White prisoners	33
Black prisoners	69
Total	102

A prison guard's hand enters the shot and changes the figures to read:

White prisoners	34
Black prisoners	69
Total	103

CAMERA PANS TO:

289. INT. OUTER ROOM SECOND PRISON CAMP

James Allen and the warden, taking in guard stationed outside the steel door.

WARDEN (to guard):

Here's that guy that all the fuss was about. If he tries to escape, shoot him.

ALLEN:

I'm supposed to be a trusty. Haven't you had orders from the prison commission?

WARDEN:

Sure, I've had orders— If you get away this time, I'll lose my job. (Turning to the guard.) So do the rest of you—get me? Go on—give him a bunk.

GUARD (to warden):

Yes, sir.

The guard grabs Allen and opens the steel door. Allen is stunned at the treatment he is receiving.

CUT TO:

290. INT. BULL PEN CLOSE SHOT

as Allen is shoved through the door. The door is

slammed shut behind him, and he stands there alone, looking around the dimly lighted room.

291. PAN SHOT
showing the faces of the convicts—some sprawling and some sitting on their beds—as they stare at the newcomer. The faces are inhumanly hard, cruel, vicious. They all stare at Allen, hostilely. Then the CAMERA REACHES one who is grinning. It is Bomber Wells. He rises.

292. FULL SHOT
as Bomber goes toward Allen.

BOMBER:
Allen—

ALLEN:
Bomber!

Bomber takes Allen's hand and shakes it. Allen is still a little stunned by his treatment from the officials.

BOMBER:
How did you get to this little bit of heaven, kid?

ALLEN:
It's a long story.

BOMBER:
You think those other chain gangs are tough—These are the guys that were *too tough* for the chain gangs. (Indicating a cot.) Sit down and make yourself at home—if you can.

Allen, moving mechanically, sits down.

BOMBER:
Now, give us the story . . . How'd they snatch you back?

ALLEN:
They didn't . . . I *came* back . . .

CONVICT:

He just got lonesome . . .

There are howls of derisive laughter from the other convicts.

ALLEN:

They promised me a pardon if I'd come back for ninety days . . .

CONVICT:

What's a "pardon"?

BOMBER (to Allen):

These boys up here ain't ever heard that word . . .

SECOND CONVICT:

Neither has the prison commission . . .

ALLEN (after a moment):

What'd *you* do to get sent up here, Bomber?

BOMBER:

Well, I decided to hang it on the limb—so I socked a guard with a sledge . . . I swung at the rat's head—(He finishes disgustedly.) But I missed . . . (He spits through his teeth.)

A CONVICT:

I can't figure a guy walking back into this just because they promised to spring him in ninety days.

ALLEN (grimly):

They just want to make it tough on me, I guess—but I'll get the pardon, all right . . .

CONVICT (to Allen):

Listen, Babe—they ain't thinkin' of givin' away pardons when you land in here. This is the last word. (He grins hideously.) You might say it's IT.

FADE OUT

FADE IN

293. A HIGHWAY

The eastern horizon has just begun to glow. The figure of a guard rises in the foreground, silhouetted black against the horizon.

GUARD:

All right—get to work.

The figures of the convicts appear out of the darkness now, all silhouetted black against the glowing east.

294. CLOSE-UP A LARGE NEGRO

He throws back his head, and from his throat come the deep tones of a Negro song. A chorus of Negro throats takes it up. Sledges start to rise and fall to the tempo of the song. The sun rises beautifully in the east—the tempo of the song mounts.

295. ALLEN

as he swings his sledge for the first time, back at hard labor in the chain gang now.

DISSOLVE TO:

296. THE HIGHWAY

The hot sun beats down. The Negro song goes on, and the work goes on, sledges swinging to the swing of the song—all in perfect synchronization with the music—an uncanny, mechanical precision.

297. ALLEN

As he swings his sledge his suffering shows on his face. He isn't used to hard labor anymore. He gets out of step with the song. There is a guard standing in front of him and he doesn't dare to quit.

GUARD:

Come on—keep the lick.

Allen gets in step with the song again.

DISSOLVE TO:

298. HIGHWAY

In the west there is a beautiful sunset, and as at dawn the figures of the convicts are seen silhouetted against it. The work and the song still go on—there is still the synchronization, but the tempo is slower now, the hymn more mournful.

GUARD:

Quit work—

The work stops. The men drag heavily toward the Ford trucks.

299. ALLEN

as he drags his body, aching with weariness and caked with sweat and road dust, toward the truck. He is almost ready to collapse. He moves slowly, his chain clanking.[66]

FADE OUT

FADE IN

300. INT. HEARING ROOM OF PRISON COMMISSION

The three prison commissioners sit behind a long, bare table. Their faces are cold and inscrutable. THE CAMERA MOVES BACK and we see the small, bare room. There are a number of people there—Ramsey, Allen's brother, the Reverend Robert Allen, newspapermen, witnesses. The chairman raps for order.

CHAIRMAN:

The case of James Allen. Is Mr. Ramsey present?

RAMSEY (rising):

Ready, Your Honor.

CHAIRMAN:

Please be brief—we've got a great number of cases this afternoon.

RAMSEY:

I should first like to introduce the convict's brother, the Reverend Robert Allen.

The Reverend Mr. Allen rises. He is dressed as a clergyman. His voice is very low as he starts to speak.

301. CLOSE-UP OF REV. ALLEN

REV. ALLEN:

I shall leave the legal technicalities of the case to Mr. Ramsey and shall present the story of James Allen as a human being—a man of essential fineness and integrity of character—a man decorated for bravery in the World War—a man who committed a crime only when forced to at the point of a gun—his first and only offense—a man who proved his real character by rising from less than nothing to become a prominent and honored citizen—

While he is saying this, DOUBLE-EXPOSED over the CLOSE-UP is a phantasmagoria of flashes of scenes of Allen's past life: again he is receiving his war decoration; he is being pursued by the police after the lunch counter robbery; he is being sentenced by the judge to a term with the chain gang.

DISSOLVE INTO:

302. EXT. HIGHWAY MED. CLOSE-UP OF JAMES ALLEN
swinging a pick on the highway, along with the other convicts, to the rhythm of a Negro's song.

DISSOLVE TO:

303. INT. HEARING ROOM
SHOT of Ramsey and the three police commissioners. Their faces are hard and cold. Ramsey is summing up the case.

RAMSEY:

And in conclusion, I need not remind you that James Allen has kept his part of the bargain. He has returned voluntarily to this state and has paid all the expenses demanded of him. I cannot believe, in the light of all this evidence and in the name of justice, that you will bring yourselves even to consider any other alternative.

Through this entire CLOSE-UP there is DOUBLE-EXPOSED a phantasmagoria of scene flashes: Allen getting off the train on his return to the chain gang state, his paying the checks to the lawyer.

304. CLOSE-UP OF CHAIRMAN

He rises and starts to speak.

CHAIRMAN:

First, I feel it is my duty to answer the malicious and unwarranted attack upon the chain gang system that we have heard this afternoon. Crime must be punished. The men who commit crimes are hard men, and their punishment must be hard. The brutality of which you hear is a gross exaggeration, born of the fancy of the uninformed. The life of the convict on a chain gang is one of hard labor—the discipline is strict—but there is no brutality. Further, the purpose of prison is not only to punish crime, but to discourage it. There is less crime in this state in proportion to its population than in forty other states in the Union. Finally, as evidence of the chain gang's value as a character builder, I have only to present to you the very case you have presented to us today—the case of James Allen, who entered the chain gang as a worthless tramp and who left it to become one of a great city's most successful and respected citizens. (He pauses and clears his throat.) The commission will take the case of James Allen under consideration.

Throughout this scene is DOUBLE-EXPOSED a phantasmagoria of different flashes of chain gang life: Red being beaten, men working on the road, bloodhounds, sledges, lashings, scum for food, and throughout is the monotonous sound of sledges.[67]

FADE OUT

FADE IN

305. INT. PRISON WAITING ROOM

The Reverend Mr. Allen is talking to his brother.

REV. ALLEN:

They refused to pardon you, Jim.

For a moment Allen is completely stunned.

ALLEN:

They refused—the state's promise didn't mean anything— (With growing anger.) It was all lies—they just wanted to get me back—to keep me here for nine more years— Their crimes are worse than mine—worse than anybody's here— They're the ones that ought to be in prison.

REV. ALLEN:

You won't have to stay the nine years, Jim. The commission voted that if you were a model prisoner for one year, the state would consider you had paid your obligation in full.

ALLEN:

Nine more months of this torture? I won't do it—I'll break out of here—if they kill me it's better than staying—

REV. ALLEN:

It's still better to be honorably free. In those nine months we'll be working for you night and day.

ALLEN:

You've *been* working day and night—it doesn't do any good.

REV. ALLEN:

We'll have the whole country behind you then—the state will be forced to release you.

ALLEN (after a moment; bitterly):

All right—I'll wait nine months—I'll be a model prisoner—if it kills me.

The Reverend Mr. Allen pats his brother's shoulder. The Negro spiritual, heard from the distance throughout the scene, rises in a crescendo of misery.

FADE OUT

FADE IN

INSERT as a sledgehammer hits a calendar and the leaves of one year fall off. Blood is spilled on the pages.

DISSOLVE INTO:

306. INT. HEARING ROOM OF PRISON COMMISSION

Ramsey is talking. The three commissioners sit with cold, emotionless faces.

RAMSEY:

. . . and finally not only has James Allen been a model prisoner—patient and uncomplaining, for a whole year—but we have presented letters from countless organizations and prominent individuals, beseeching you to recommend his pardon. I think it only just, Your Honors, that he be granted his freedom while there is still time for him to regain his former position in society, of prominence and universal respect.

The faces of the commissioners are unchanged, still stony and inscrutable.

FADE OUT

FADE IN

307. BULLPEN NIGHT

The men lie sprawled on their beds, exhausted. The warden enters, with the leather strap in his hand that he uses to beat the men with. A guard accompanies him.

As the warden passes the foot of Allen's bunk he pauses.

WARDEN (to Allen):

We've just had a final report on your new hearing.

ALLEN (gazing up at him, tense and rigid):

Well . . . ?

WARDEN:

They've suspended decision indefinitely. (He continues along the row of bunks; then, toying with the leather strap, he turns to the guard.) Which one, did they say?

GUARD (pointing to a convict lying on his bunk):

That one there.

WARDEN (to convict):

Get up—you lazy skunk.

308. CLOSE-UP OF ALLEN'S HAND

clutching the iron frame of his bunk convulsively. CAMERA PANS UP to his face, which is barely recognizable. It is cruel, distorted, inhuman.

FADE OUT

NOTE: From this point until the final fade out, Allen is like an animal. He is shifty, cringing, silent. His eyes are wild, and he seems to be all eyes.

FADE IN

309. EXT. HIGHWAY

The convicts at work. James Allen and Bomber Wells stand on opposite sides of the road, waiting with shovels in their hands. Twenty feet ahead of them two other convicts stand waiting, a guard beside them. A truck drives past between Allen and Bomber and stops just past the next two convicts. The driver pulls a lever; the front end of the loaded part of the truck rises slowly, dumping out the dirt. The two convicts start spreading out the dirt, and the guard moves down to Allen and Bomber. The driver lowers the truck again and drives off.

Allen, his bitter face tense, gives Bomber a look. Bomber answers with a barely perceptible nod.

Another truck drives up and stops just past Bomber

and Allen. The driver pulls the lever, and the front of the loaded part of the body rises. The driver looks out the window back of the seat until he is hidden completely by the rising body. The dirt slides out onto the road.

Allen has apparently discovered something wrong under the truck.

ALLEN:

Hey, driver—better take a look back here.

The driver sticks his head out the side of the driver's seat.

DRIVER:

I haven't got time—I got some stuff here to rush up to the quarry . . .

ALLEN:

You'll never make the quarry in this truck—your spring's broken . . .

The driver gets off the seat and comes back to the rear of the truck.

ALLEN:

Look under there . . . (He points in behind the rear wheel.)

Both the guard and the driver get down on their hands and knees to look under the truck.

Allen and Bomber sneak quickly to the front of the truck and climb on. The motor is still running. There is a box on the front seat. Allen releases the brake and starts the truck. It leaps ahead.

The guard and the driver look up surprised as the truck drives off from over them. Allen shifts again and the truck roars ahead. The guard jumps to his feet, grabbing up a gun and starting to shoot. Another guard runs up and shoots.

A SERIES OF QUICK CUTS

310. ALLEN
shifts again and the truck roars ahead down the road. The bullets rattle off the raised back of the truck.

311. THE GUARDS
One of them blows his whistle. The others start rounding up the convicts.

312. ANOTHER GUARD
further down the road. He blows his whistle.

313. A STEAM WHISTLE
It starts screeching loudly.

314. ROAD
Another truck drives up. One of the guards jumps on it and it starts after Allen's truck.

315. ALLEN'S TRUCK
It is going as fast as it can now, twenty-five miles an hour.

316. ALLEN AND BOMBER
in the front seat. The big box is in their way.

ALLEN:
Throw the box out.

BOMBER:
Nix. It's full of my favorite candy.

Allen darts a glance at the box.

317. INSERT
Sign on the box: Dynamite

318. ALLEN AND BOMBER
Bomber grins.

319. PRISON YARD

The steam whistle is screeching. An auto filled with guards and guns dashes out and down the road.

320. ALLEN'S TRUCK

going along the highway.

ALLEN:

It won't go any faster. All these trucks have got governors that hold them down to twenty-five . . .

BOMBER (looks outside):

There's nothing in sight yet—stop the truck.

Allen brings the truck to a stop. Bomber jumps out, rips open the hood, and takes off the governor.[68] Allen pulls the lever that lowers the back of the truck. Another motor is heard.

321. LONG SHOT

The second truck tears around a corner.

322. ALLEN'S TRUCK

as Bomber jumps on and Allen drives off.

323. ROAD

A touring car full of guards and bristling with guns speeds past the second truck. Its siren is screaming.

324. ALLEN'S TRUCK

going much faster now. The scream of the siren is heard faintly above the roar of the motor.

325. SECOND TOURING CAR

A different make but full of men and guns, speeding along a different road.[69]

326. FARMHOUSE BY HIGHWAY

The scream of the steam whistle is heard. A farmer runs

out of the house with a gun. Allen's truck tears past and the farmer takes a quick shot. The truck roars on.

327. ALLEN'S TRUCK
The screams of the sirens are loud now. Bomber starts tearing open the box of dynamite.

328. SECOND TOURING CAR
coming along a dirt road. One of the men in the tonneau points.

329. LONG SHOT FROM MOVING CAR
of Allen's truck speeding along a highway at right angles to the dirt road.

330. ALLEN'S TRUCK
Bomber and Allen see the touring car on the dirt road, very close.

331. SECOND TOURING CAR
The men start shooting.

332. ALLEN'S TRUCK
A fusillade of shots strikes it. Bomber grabs at his chest. A spot of blood appears. Bomber's face becomes vicious and he pulls a stick of dynamite out of the box.

333. INTERSECTION OF ROADS
The touring car skids around the turn and takes the highway, after the truck.

334. ALLEN'S TRUCK
Allen pulls the lever that raises the back. Bomber is fastening a cap and fuse to a stick of dynamite.

335. THE ROAD
The second touring car is gaining fast on the truck. The men start shooting again. Another car is close behind the second touring car.

336. ALLEN'S TRUCK

The back is raised just in time. The bullets rattle off. Bomber has the fuse lighted now.

ALLEN:

They're right on our tail.

Bomber nods. The spot of blood on his chest is larger now. Suddenly he swings out on the step of the truck and throws the dynamite. There is the sound of a terrific explosion, and the truck is almost thrown off the road. Bomber breaks into a scream of wild laughter.

BOMBER:

That's once I didn't miss.[70]

Bomber grabs suddenly at his chest, hangs a moment, then falls off the truck.

337. HIGHWAY

Bomber's body rolls into the ditch at the side of the road and lies still. He is dead.

338. HIGHWAY

The cloud of smoke and dust from the explosion stops the following touring car full of guards.

DISSOLVE TO:

339. A BRIDGE

Allen's truck drives across the bridge and stops.

340. CLOSE SHOT TRUCK

Allen looks back. There is nothing in sight. He swings his legs back over the driver's seat and puts the chains across the heavy steel cog.

341. CLOSE-UP OF THE COGS

Allen's chained legs enter the SHOT, one foot on either side of the massive cogs, so that the chain which connects his legs lies caught in the cogs. He reaches back and pulls the lever behind him. The machinery starts moving and the body commences to descend. As it does so the cogs grind a couple of links of the chain into powder. Allen's feet are free. He pulls them back quickly to get out of the way of the descending body.

342. CLOSE-UP
of Allen in front seat of truck. He pulls the ankle bracelets up to his knees and attaches the loose ends of the chain to the bracelets, pulling his trousers down over the chains in order to hide them. He looks back.

343. LONG SHOT
One of the touring cars comes over the crest of a hill.

344. ALLEN'S TRUCK
Allen grabs a stick out of the box and starts fixing it with cap and fuse.

345. TOURING CAR
coming on.

346. INT. TOURING CAR
One of the men points at Allen's truck on the bridge.

347. BRIDGE
Allen throws the dynamite with the fuse lighted far out on the bridge.

348. TOURING CAR
nearly to the bridge.

349. ALLEN
watching tensely.

350. MINIATURE
Just before the car reaches it, there is a tremendous explosion in the middle of the bridge. The bridge crumples and collapses.

FADE OUT

FADE IN
SERIES OF INSERTS OF NEWSPAPER HEADLINES

CONVICT MAKES SECOND ESCAPE

JAMES ALLEN AT LARGE AGAIN
Desperate Convict, Denied
Pardon, Escapes Second Time,
Dynamites Bridge.

GUNMAN ESCAPES
Authorities Confident of
Allen's Recapture.[71]

DISSOLVE TO:

351. CLOSE-UP
of a U.S. map. The CAMERA MOVES from one spot to another, hesitating, then jumping here, there, and everywhere. SUPERIMPOSED is a hodgepodge of trains, boats, and automobiles. SUPERIMPOSED on this map are the pages of a calendar—turning, turning, turning. Finally the CAMERA STOPS, IRISED on Chicago.

DISSOLVE TO:

352. AN ALLEY
A row of garages facing the alley, behind a large apartment house. A Ford coupe turns into the alley and into the open door of one of the garages. After a moment a girl comes out.

MAN'S VOICE:
Helen—

She stops and turns. Allen appears out of the darkness, slinking along the edge of the building for protection. He has on a suit that was once good but is now old and worn. He looks like a bum. Helen stares at him a moment, then gasps as she recognizes him. He draws her back into the shadows.

HELEN (her voice choking):
Jim! Jim—why haven't you come before?

ALLEN:

I couldn't! I was afraid to.

HELEN:

You could have written. It's been almost a year since you escaped!

ALLEN (with a bitter laugh):

I haven't escaped—they're still after me. They'll always be after me. I've had jobs but I can't keep them. Something happens—someone turns up—I hide in rooms all day and travel by night—no friends—no rest—no peace—

HELEN (clutching him):

Jim!

ALLEN:

Keep moving! That's all that's left for me.

HELEN (clinging to him):

No—please! I can't let you go like this. It was all going to be so different . . .[72]

ALLEN (with a hollow laugh):

I hate everything but you . . . I had to take a chance tonight to see you . . . and say good-bye . . .

Helen gazes at him with tears streaming down her face; then she throws her arms about his neck impulsively and kisses him. They cling together fiercely. There is the sound of a police siren approaching, then fading away. Allen is startled, then starts away.

HELEN (following him):

Can't you tell me where you're going? (He shakes his head.) Will you write? (He shakes his head.) Do you need any money? (He shakes his head again, still backing away.) But you must, Jim! How do you live?

A car is heard approaching. Allen backs into the dark shadows of the alley.

ALLEN:

I steal . . . [73]

Helen stands watching, an expression of infinite suffering and pity on her face, as Allen disappears into the darkness.

DISSOLVE TO:

353. CLOSE-UP

of map as in previous scene with CAMERA jumping north, south, east, west, and finally

DISSOLVING INTO:

354. THE BROW OF A HILL AT DAWN

In the shot is a sign which reads

U.S. BORDER

The figure of Allen in silhouette is seen trudging slowly up and over the brow of the hill, a broken, defeated, beaten figure of a man, a hunted animal, a fugitive. Over this come the words:

THE END

Notes to the Screenplay

Although Sheridan Gibney's name appears on the title page of the Final screenplay (page 59), he received no credit on the screen.

1 The moving-scroll Foreword was omitted from the film.
2 As an interesting touch, the camera first focuses on a spiked German helmet that a soldier is bringing home as a souvenir.
3 As part of ad lib in the breaking up of the crap game, one of the white soldiers tries to pocket the black player's dice but finally turns them over.
4 Allen's words in the film are: "I know what I'm gonna do—get me some kind of construction job." The preceding five speeches are not in the film.
5 This speech is reworded in film: "It wasn't, but it's going to be. Being in the Engineering Corps has been swell experience, and I'm making the most of it."
6 This speech is reworded in the film, possibly in reference to the German helmet in scene 2: "You can bet your little tin hat, Mr. James Allen won't be back in the old grind of a factory."
7 This shot was dropped from the film, probably for reasons of cost. The preceding stock shot stands alone and no attempt is made to pick out Allen in the crowd.
8 A sign on the station identifies the town as Lynndale.
9 Other friends do not appear in the film. The welcoming group includes only his mother, brother, girl, and employer.
10 The rest of scene 11, scenes 12 and 13, and the first part of scene 14 are deleted in the film. Instead Allen steps off the train at the door closest to the group and his mother runs directly into his arms.
11 This exchange was cut; instead, Alice soon makes the point about his not wearing his uniform. (The Final script shows revised pages, dated July 28, 1932, from this point to scene 39.)
12 Before the revisions, Parker says he has a more important job for Allen than the one he left behind. Clearly, at the last minute (July 28) this was changed to the same job to emphasize the routine of it and to avoid confusion later on when Allen describes the job as "stupid and insignificant."

Dialog is added to the end of the scene for transition to the next one, with Allen saying, "Well, I guess we'd better go home, don't you think?" and Parker replying, "See you later, Jim."

13 The rest of Allen's speech is not in the film, nor are the next two speeches.

14 Scenes 19–21 and 22 to this point are not in the film.

15 Before this entire sequence (scenes 15–22) was added in the revisions of July 28, 1932, the script called for a dissolve from the train station directly to the shoe factory. The effect of the change is to give the audience a more intimate identification with Allen. Millions of American households had gone through this same sort of homecoming.

16 In an interesting touch, this shot in the film opens with the camera focused on an unattended table setting; it then zooms out to include the mother and brother.

17 Contrary to the scripted directions, the first part of this shot leaves the camera on Clint, accentuating his pompous and sanctimonious attitude.

18 The line is omitted, as well as some in scene 32 that refer to psychological problems and a doctor.

19 The rest of the speech is not in the film. This speech was brought together, lengthened, and strengthened from a series of interchanges with the brother in an earlier version and gave Muni the opportunity to show his creative skill.

Allen's reference to dancing and being "out of step" with everyone else relates to a three-page scene deleted in the revision of July 28. It had him and Alice attending a community dance where he was laughed at for his "old-fashioned" (prewar) dancing style. Alice's comments in scene 14 on Allen's having looked more handsome and distinguished in his uniform were originally intended for this scene.

20 Scenes 39–41 are not in the film.

21 Allen's last speech and his boss's reply are not in the film. Instead Allen shows his indifference and nonchalance with an ironic "all right." Clearly he doesn't expect to have a hard time finding another job.

22 The locale of scenes 44 and 45 in the film is changed from a levee repair crew to some sort of a factory or mill. No Negroes are evident.

23 In the film Allen can be seen asleep on the undercarriage of the freight car.

24 In the flophouse no Negroes are evident. Other men are in the

background, but there is no real focus on them. Instead of sitting, Allen is leaning against a post and watching Pete play solitaire.

25 The reference to his Hispano-Suize is changed to a Rolls-Royce in the film. Pete's next line and the two speeches that follow are not in the film. Instead Pete asks simply, "What's your name?"

26 In the film, the rest of scene 60 and all of scenes 60–67 (the entire chase sequence) are deleted. Instead Allen is captured by two cops immediately outside the door of the diner. One cop sticks his gun in Allen's belly:

FIRST COP: Put 'em up. Thought you'd get away, huh?

ALLEN: But I didn't do nothin'.

SECOND COP: Oh, no?

ALLEN: No . . . No!

27 In the film, a blip made by the sound of the gavel obliterates one word of the judge's sentence so it is not clear for how many years Allen is to be sent away.

28 Now there is a dissolve to a shot panning the prison yard and bleak-looking wooden camp buildings. The camera also shows a sign, County Camp No. 2, before returning to the blacksmith's shop and focusing on him counting the links in Allen's chains.

29 In the film, "To put in your nose!" The rest of scene 70 and all of 71 are not in the film. Instead, the guard escorts him from the blacksmith shop with "All right, take it out. Follow me," and the shot closes with a fade out.

30 The scene fades in with a superimposed title: 4:20 A.M. The guard's yelling for the men to get up is replaced with the incessant clanging of a triangle. More vocal orders of guards are added, however, and they are barked in staccato fashion, in vicious and angry tones: "All right—pick 'em up. (Referring to rings on their chains.) Come on—pull 'em through. All right—stand off. (To Allen.) That'll learn you to sit up and hold onto this! All right, you guys—get goin' there. Get those shoes on—get up. Come on—hurry it up. (To Allen.) Pick up that chain."

31 In the film, this shot is photographed from the floor, accentuating the men dragging their feet and the noise made by the chains.

32 In the film, Allen has no utensils. Bomber Wells, seated next to him, pushes toward him a spoon, which Allen wipes with his fingers before digging in. Thus Bomber's character is friendly and helpful from the moment we first meet him.

33 In the film the cutting of the shots at the breakfast table is interesting. Most shots are straight on, at eye level, putting the viewer in

the place of a convict rather than a guard. Most shots are of one person, emphasizing the agony of the individual prisoner. The conversation is surly and generally unfriendly. There is one interesting three-shot that does give the sense of a community around the table when Barney responds to Bomber about the coffee with Allen listening in. But it is evident that Allen is the only real human being there. Not yet broken by camp life himself, he pities the others, especially Red. Muni's acting ability is especially evident here.

34 In the film the warden cannot be distinguished from the guards. The order in the film is changed to: "Come on, move out."

35 A touch on the arm would be too personal. In the film Nordine taps Allen on the back with the handle of his pickax.

36 Nordine follows his speech with a weird, insane kind of giggle.

37 Allen's reply is instead ironic and resentful: "For looking at a hamburger."

38 The start of the workday is signaled in the film by a whistle, reminiscent of the factory call at Kumfort Shoes and the ship's whistle at the beginning of the film.

39 In the film we see the guard walk up to Allen and punch him squarely in the jaw, rather than seeing just a fist enter the screen. Allen doesn't reach for his sledge to go after the guard until after he turns his back.

40 Instead of pulling back and taking in the entire chain gang, the camera moves in even closer on Red.

41 Water is thrown, but there is no kick.

42 The film adds a superimposed title: 8:20 P. M. An eerie light is shed on the prison yard by four or five men holding open-flame lamps (like smudge pots) attached to the top of six-foot poles. Evidently these were suggested on the set by LeRoy's consultants who had previous experience with prison camps.

43 This is an establishing shot for a later scene where suspense is generated about whether the guard would notice that Allen's shackles had been bent out of shape. This was one of the specific shots Zanuck suggested in his story conference of June 7, 1932. Allen, unfamiliar with the routine, has to be ordered to "spread 'em out."

44 Scene 102 and this shot are not in the film.

45 Scenes 117–20 are changed somewhat in the film. The guard tears off Ackerman's shirt and throws it on his cot. We see the shadow of the warden with the whip as it crashes on Ackerman's back, and the camera stays on Allen until Ackerman's whipping is done. Acker-

man stumbles, bleeding, to his own cot and the warden's line about his shirt is deleted. The camera shows four or five convicts, closes on Ackerman's bloody back, and never reaches the door.

46 As Barney walks strangely toward the prison gate the camera passes without special notice a man tied to two crossed stakes—an obvious reference to a form of crucifixion.

47 As Red's coffin is hoisted onto the truck we see via double exposure a replay of the earlier scene where he had passed out and had a bucket of water thrown in his face.

48 Accenting Red's insignificance in death as in life, Barney strikes a match against Red's coffin to light his cigarette.

49 Here Allen adds, "You hit it when you can." Sebastian's next two speeches are reversed in order; Allen's last speech is only "I promise."

50 As the unleashed dogs begin yelping the sound of a loud steam whistle is introduced. The sound is like a locomotive but is evidently meant to represent the chain gang's escape alarm. It persists through the following six or seven shots and adds to the tension.

51 This entire underwater sequence had been suggested in Zanuck's conference notes of June 7, 1932. In the first underwater shot of Allen (175) tell-tale bubbles are seen on top of the water, but the pursuing guard does not notice them. Eventually a guard plunges into the water too and is seen in an underwater shot poking around near Allen. Scenes 179–84 are not in the film, which dissolves directly from the swamp to the city.

52 The sign in the film is I. Gollober: Classy Clothes. In the next shot the haberdasher observes, "You look like a new man," and Allen buys a "cheap hat" to complete his new wardrobe.

53 An interesting setup for a shot, for whatever reason it does not appear in the film. As Allen's chair springs up straight we are looking at him eye to eye.

54 The hat is not a prison issue (see note 52), and instead of dropping it, Allen pulls it down over the right side of his forehead (the side facing the policeman) as he walks toward the door. The film omits scenes 196–99 so that Allen is seen leaving the barbershop and immediately taking out the slip with Barney's address that Bomber had given him.

55 This scene is not in the film.

56 The dialogue now skips to scene 209 where Linda sits on the bed, puts her hand on Allen's knee, and says, "If there's anything I can do . . ."

57 Scene 215 immediately follows in the film.

58 In the film Allen already has his hand on the door of the train when the shout "There he is" is heard. His face contorts in terror, but it cannot be seen by the lawmen. As the police chase a hobo from beneath the train they pass the doorway where he is cringing in fear.

59 Of scenes 234–42, the film includes only 238–40 and accompanies those with a superimposed map to indicate movement from the Southeast to Chicago.

60 Note the irony of his job with pick and shovel after escape from the chain gang—but now he is free. He can even wipe the sweat from his face without having to ask permission.

61 The film telescopes Allen's rise. By this time he is assistant superintendent at fourteen dollars per day (a surveyor at twelve dollars in the preceding scene). The scene that follows is not in the film.

62 Dialogue is expanded in the film to make ironic reference to Allen's experiences and to his sense of being trapped by Marie. Helen asks, "What do you like to do?" and Allen replies, "Build bridges and roads for people to use when they want to get away from things. But they can't get away. Nobody can." This, of course, was tame compared with the irony written into earlier versions of the script that called for a floor show at the club with chorus girls (including Helen) dressed in scanty costumes and playing at being on a chain gang.

Scenes 264–68 precede the scene in the club so that Allen is aware of his wife's infidelity before he meets Helen.

63 Scenes 260–63 are deleted from the film. Instead we see a long shot of men constructing a bridge with a superimposed calendar showing the passage of several months' time. Film fades to shot 269.

64 Scenes 277–80 were deleted from the film, presumably to save time (277–78 are implied later on) and expense (for example, the banquet setup).

65 In place of the station scene, the film shows a stock shot of a train passing and superimposes a map moving to the Southeast. Action dissolves directly to the attorney's office.

66 This shot is not in the film, and in 293–98 the orders of the guards are deleted, leaving as the only sound the crashing of the picks and sledges and the poignant song.

67 The superimpositions here and at the same point in scenes 301 and 303 are not in the film.

68 The business about stopping the truck to remove the governor is not in the film.

69 The second touring car does not appear in the film.

70 Bomber adds the last, ironic words, "Gettin' out here." More important, Bomber doesn't fall until after Allen crosses the bridge (scene 339). The film emphasizes the loyalty between Allen and Bomber by having Allen stop the truck to check on his fallen friend before removing his chain and blowing up the bridge.

71 The film used more headlines and newspaper story inserts than the script called for. Instead of scene 351, calendar pages are superimposed here to indicate the passage of one year's time.

72 This speech follows Allen's next one, and he replies, "It is different—they've made it different."

73 The film ends here with music rising in volume.

Production Credits

Directed by	Mervyn LeRoy
Screenplay by	Howard J. Green and Brown Holmes
Edited by	William Holmes
Art Director	Jack Okey
Photography by	Sol Polito
Gowns by	Orry-Kelly
Technical Director	S. H. Sullivan
Silks by	Cheney Brothers
Vitaphone Orchestra conducted by	Leo F. Forbstein

Released: November 1932
Running time: 93 minutes

Cast

James Allen	Paul Muni
Marie	Glenda Farrell
Helen	Helen Vinson
Linda	Noel Francis
Pete	Preston Foster
Barney Sykes	Allen Jenkins
Bomber Wells	Edward Ellis
Nordine	John Wray
Sebastian	Everett Brown
The Reverend Robert Allen	Hale Hamilton
Mother	Louise Carter
Alice	Sally Blane
Judge	Berton Churchill
Warden	David Landau
Prison Board Chairman	Willard Robertson
Attorney	Robert McWade
Fuller	Robert Warwick

Inventory

The following materials from the Warner library of the Wisconsin Center for Film and Theater Research were used by O'Connor in preparing *I Am a Fugitive from a Chain Gang* for the Wisconsin/Warner Bros. Screenplay Series:

I Am a Fugitive from a Georgia Chain Gang!, by Robert E. Burns. New York: Vanguard, 1932. 257 pages.
Outline, no author shown, April 15, 1932. 16 pages.
Treatment, by Brown Holmes. April 23, 1932. 86 pages.
Screenplay, by Sheridan Gibney. No date. 132 pages.
Temporary, by Gibney and Holmes. May 31, 1932. 144 pages.
Screenplay, by Howard J. Green. July 19, 1932.
Final, by Green, Holmes, and Gibney. July 23 with revisions to July 28, 1932. 143 pages.

DESIGNED BY GARY GORE
COMPOSED BY THE NORTH CENTRAL PUBLISHING COMPANY
ST. PAUL, MINNESOTA
MANUFACTURED BY INTER-COLLEGIATE PRESS, INC.
SHAWNEE MISSION, KANSAS
TEXT AND DISPLAY LINES ARE SET IN PALATINO

Library of Congress Cataloging in Publication Data
Green, Howard, J.
I am a fugitive from a chain gang.
(Wisconsin/Warner Bros. screenplay series)
Screenplay by Howard J. Green, Brown Holmes, and Sheridan Gibney,
based on the book by Robert Elliott Burns.
Includes bibliographical references.
I. O'Connor, John E. II. Holmes, Brown. III. Gibney, Sheridan.
IV. Burns, Robert Elliott. I am a fugitive from a Georgia chain gang.
V. I am a fugitive from a chain gang.
VI. Title. VII. Series.
PN1997.I13 791.43'72 81-50823
ISBN 0-299-08750-6 AACR2
ISBN 0-299-08754-9 (pbk.)

WW

WISCONSIN / WARNER BROS SCREENPLAY SERIES

The Wisconsin/Warner Bros. Screenplay Series, a product of the Warner Brothers Film Library of the University of Wisconsin-Madison, offers scholars, students, researchers, and aficionados insights into individual films that have never before been possible.

The Warner library was acquired in 1957 by the United Artists Corporation, which in turn donated it to the Wisconsin Center for Film and Theater Research in 1969. The massive library, housed in the State Historical Society of Wisconsin, contains eight hundred sound feature films, fifteen hundred short subjects, and nineteen thousand still negatives, as well as the legal files, press books, and screenplays of virtually every Warner film produced from 1930 until 1950. This rich treasure trove has made the University of Wisconsin one of the major centers for film research, attracting scholars from around the world. This series of published screenplays represents a creative use of the Warner library, both a boon to scholars and a tribute to United Artists.

Most published film scripts are literal transcriptions of finished films. The Wisconsin/Warner screenplays are primary source documents—the final shooting versions including revisions made during production. As such, they reveal the art of screenwriting as other film transcriptions cannot. Comparing these screenplays with the final films will illuminate the arts of directing and acting, as well as the other arts of the film making process. (Films of the Warner library are available at modest rates from the United Artists nontheatrical rental library, United Artists/16 mm.)

From the eight hundred feature films in the library, the editors of the series selected for publication examples that have received critical recognition for excellence of directing, screenwriting, and acting, films distinctive in genre, in historical relevance, and in adaptation of well-known novels and plays.